Stop Worrying

Stop Worrying

Get your life back on track with CBT

Ad Kerkhof

In collaboration with
Saida Akhnikh, Anneke Koopman, Maarten van der Linde,
Marleen Stam & Elvan Tutkun

 Open University Press

Open University Press
McGraw-Hill Education
McGraw-Hill House
Shoppenhangers Road
Maidenhead
Berkshire
England
SL6 2QL

email: enquiries@openup.co.uk
world wide web: www.openup.co.uk

and Two Penn Plaza, New York, NY 10121–2289, USA

Piekeren, First edition, by Ad J. F. M. Kerkhof
Original edition copyright 2007 by Boom uitgevers. All rights reserved

English language of Piekeren by Ad J. F. M. Kerkhof
First edition copyright 2010 by Open University Press. All rights reserved.

English translation copyright © Anna George, 2010

A catalogue record of this book is available from the British Library

ISBN-13: 978–0–33–524252–8
ISBN-10: 0–33–524252–9

Library of Congress Cataloging-in-Publication Data
CIP data applied for

Typeset by RefineCatch Limited, Bungay, Suffolk
Printed in the UK by Bell and Bain Ltd, Glasgow

Fictitious names of companies, products, people, characters and/or data that may be used herein (in case studies or in examples) are not intended to represent any real individual, company, product or event.

Mixed Sources
Product group from well-managed
forests and other controlled sources
www.fsc.org   Cert no. TT-COC-002769
© 1996 Forest Stewardship Council

	never	very rarely	rarely	some-times	often	very often	almost always
10 I did not worry about anything.	6	5	4	3	2	1	0
11 When there was nothing more I could do about a concern, I did not worry about it any more.	6	5	4	3	2	1	0
12 I noticed that I had been worrying about things.	0	1	2	3	4	5	6
13 Once I started worrying, I couldn't stop.	0	1	2	3	4	5	6
14 I worried all the time.	0	1	2	3	4	5	6
15 I worried about projects until they were all done.	0	1	2	3	4	5	6
Total							

➠ *Total score for the second week:*

A word in the meantime

Worry is a reaction to a threat. People and animals react in much the same way to a threat. One option is to fight. The other option is flight. Worrying is not really either of the two. Excessive worrying is getting stuck at the preparation stage. No decision is made. All options are chewed over again and again. No solutions arise from this. You are not fleeing or fighting – it's as though you've frozen.

Postponement   It is important for you to learn how to postpone your worrying, otherwise you will be inclined to give in to it. These worrying thoughts will then take all your attention and concentration. If you just worry during the worry time, then it's easier to find solutions to your problems outside this time.

Writing exercises   In the coming two weeks we are going to concentrate on your thinking habits. We are going to tackle those worries with a number of writing exercises. You have everything you need to practise this to hand. It does not matter what you write, what matters is that you write something. You can write what you want. Spelling, grammar and sentence structure are not important. Writing exercises call for imagination. Worries are always fantasies – negative fantasies about how it will all go wrong. But you can also use fantasy to imagine how fantastically well things can go! We are now going to combat negative fantasies (worries) with positive and realistic fantasies.

Week

2

What are you worrying about?   You could be worrying about an event in the future. You might think of a number of possible scenarios for how things could turn out and what the best thing is for you to do. You could also be worrying about the past. Perhaps you wanted something to have turned out differently, or wish you had reacted differently in the situation. If you are in an uncertain situation, it can sometimes be difficult to actually come to a decision. You keep on having doubts and asking yourself what would be the right choice.

But what does worrying actually achieve? By worrying you probably just end up feeling more tense, with more doubts and no solutions or decisions. Perhaps you will benefit more if you worry less in similar situations.

Week 3

Day 15 *Writing exercise*

Worry time I
Worry intensely
morning/afternoon

Explanation   We all know that feeling well – you worry and feel anxious. This can be relieved by writing down your worries so that you get your thoughts in order. By putting your feelings into writing you can free yourself of worry.

a   Begin with five minutes intense worrying.

b   Then get out your pen and paper, or use a notebook. Write down your worries and feelings in as much detail as possible. If nothing comes to mind, then you can also use yesterday's worries.

In the meantime   If you worry during the day you can choose from one of the following exercises to reduce this: positive worrying, whirling exercise, clouds or look for some distraction.

Worry time II
Core thoughts
evening

a   Begin with ten minutes intense worrying.

b   Then look at what you have written this morning or this afternoon. This can help you rank your thoughts in order of importance.
    Some worries can look unimportant when you read them back but some may just reflect core thoughts. Core thoughts

are the thoughts which always keep coming back to trouble you whenever you worry.

c   Write down at least three core thoughts below on this page of the book.

At night   When you lie in bed and think about what you have got planned for the next day? When you think for example what do you have to do? Change the meaning: '*I must . . .*' to '*I want . . .*' When you have done that then you can in your imagination, try to put the worries into the shoebox or the rucksack under the bed where they will then stay . . . Let them stay there until the next day. Then the following morning you can bring out your anxieties and look at them again.

Core thoughts

1   ....

....

....

2   ....

....

....

3   ....

....

....

28
27
26
25
24
23
22
21
20
19
18
17
16
15
14
13
12
11
10
9
8
7
6
5
4
3
2
1

Day 15 Notes

1   Tick the boxes to indicate which subjects you have worried about today (you can give several answers).

studies/ work	finances	health	relationships	family/ friends	what others think of me	other
❏	❏	❏	❏	❏	❏	❏

2   Tick a box to indicate how many minutes/hours you have worried today.

0–30 minutes	30–60 minutes	1–2 hours	2–3 hours	3–4 hours	4–5 hours	> 5 hours
❏	❏	❏	❏	❏	❏	❏

3   Tick a box to indicate how much effort it took today to stop worrying, on a scale of 1 (almost no effort) to 5 (a great deal of effort).

no effort at all	almost no effort	some effort	quite a lot of effort	a great deal of effort
❏	❏	❏	❏	❏

4 How did you sleep last night? Indicate to what extent the following three statements apply to you.

	completely true	true	neutral	untrue	not true at all
I found it hard to get to sleep.	1	2	3	4	5
I suffered disturbed or broken sleep.	1	2	3	4	5
I awoke too early.	1	2	3	4	5

5 **Event** Did anything particular happen today which made you start to worry? If so then write down what happened below, using key words.

....

....

....

....

....

....

....

....

....

28
27
26
25
24
23
22
21
20
19
18
17
16
15
14
13
12
11
10
9
8
7
6
5
4
3
2
1

Day 16 *Three-scenarios writing exercise*

Worry time I
Fantasy
morning/afternoon

Step 1   You have already done this exercise on days 10–12. You are going to do it once again but this time more quickly. This exercise is handy for when you get anxious about future events.

Write down the most important worries of the moment in a notebook. For example: 'I am afraid I am not going to manage on my salary and that I won't be able to pay my bills any more' or 'I can't go to my parents to ask for money again, they'll just throw me out'.

Week
3

Step 2   Look at this worry like a film. Now write the future in the style of a really disastrous scenario. What is the worst that can happen? Use your imagination and exaggerate. For example: 'If I go home and ask my parents for money again, then they won't want to give me any more, because I have spent so much. And then I won't be able to go on holiday with my friends. They will then talk to me about my spending patterns and reduce what they pay me each month to help out. I am afraid that they will stop supporting me financially altogether and that I must get a job. And without the education I have missed out on I will never be able to find an interesting career. So I shall have to make do with stacking shelves at the supermarket for the rest of my life. My parents will be so angry at my request that they will throw me out.'

In the meantime   There is one more exercise you can do in the meantime when you worry. Clap your hands and say to yourself. 'Not now!'

Worry time II
Future scenario
evening

Step 3   Now write a future scenario which is as positive as possible. Try to make the situation exactly as you want it. Use your imagination and try to make it as lifelike as you can. You can exaggerate, however odd your ideas may seem. It is after all fantasy and not reality.

For example: 'When I go home to ask my parents for money to go on holiday, they will be completely happy about this. They say they prefer I ask them for money rather than having to go and earn it at the supermarket. They say they prefer I spend my time studying rather than working on extra jobs. In addition they say that they are pleased they are able to support me. They say that I should never be too embarrassed to call upon them for help.'

Step 4   Now that you have written down a positive scenario and a negative scenario you should now write a scenario that is mid-way between step 2 and step 3. This is probably the most realistic scenario.

At night   Try to postpone your worries until the next worry time. Look for some distraction or try to do positive worrying 1 (day 1) about a good memory or positive worrying 2 (day 2) about a good quality.

28
27
26
25
24
23
22
21
20
19
18
17
16
15
14
13
12
11
10
9
8
7
6
5
4
3
2
1

Day 16 Notes

Week

3

1   Tick the boxes to indicate which subjects you have worried about today (you can give several answers).

studies/ work	finances	health	relationships	family/ friends	what others think of me	other
❑	❑	❑	❑	❑	❑	❑

2   Tick a box to indicate how many minutes/hours you have worried today.

0–30 minutes	30–60 minutes	1–2 hours	2–3 hours	3–4 hours	4–5 hours	> 5 hours
❑	❑	❑	❑	❑	❑	❑

3   Tick a box to indicate how much effort it took today to stop worrying, on a scale of 1 (almost no effort) to 5 (a great deal of effort).

no effort at all	almost no effort	some effort	quite a lot of effort	a great deal of effort
❑	❑	❑	❑	❑

4 How did you sleep last night? Indicate to what extent the following three statements apply to you.

	completely true	true	neutral	untrue	not true at all
I found it hard to get to sleep.	1	2	3	4	5
I suffered disturbed or broken sleep.	1	2	3	4	5
I awoke too early.	1	2	3	4	5

5 **Event** Did anything particular happen today which made you start to worry? If so then write down what happened below, using key words.

....

....

....

....

....

....

....

....

....

Day 17 *Scoring*

Worry time I
Scoring task
morning/afternoon

Explanation   How often do you have your tiresome worrying thoughts now? Worries often go through your head unnoticed. This exercise will teach you to be aware of the extent to which you worry. You may be a bit shocked at the results. But just bear in mind that you can only tackle your behaviour in terms of worrying if you are aware of it.

a   Begin with five minutes intense worrying.

b   Today's exercise is scoring. Write down now which worry is most significant at this point in time. Which worry is going through your head most? Which worry always keeps recurring? You wlll need a notebook and a pen or pencil for this exercise. Keep this with you during the day, in your bag or on your desk, for example. Every time you notice you are having this worry again make a short line in the notebook. You will score your worry until the second worry time.

c   We will come back to this scoring exercise in the second worry time.

In the meantime   Try to postpone your worries until the next worry time. If this does not work then look for a distraction but remember to continue scoring.

Worry time II
Purposeful worrying?
evening

a Begin with five minutes intense worrying.

b Your task for today was to score one of your worries. Now count the number of lines on the page. How frequently did you have this worry?

Now ask yourself what you gained from this worry. What did you get out of it? Did it give you any relief or did this thought just end up making you feel more tense? Did it make you any wiser? Did you come to any conclusions?

Then divide the number of lines you have written down by two. If you have had this worry in total 32 times, for example, 32 divided by 2 is 16. Tomorrow's task is to halve the number of time you have this worry: try to have this worry not more than 16 times instead of 32 times.

At night If you can't sleep, try the whirling exercise again, or one of the other fantasy exercises from this book – choose the one which works best for you.

At the top of the following page, write your top 3 worries for the last day in key words. Choose one of these three worries and score this one until the next worry time tomorrow. As with today's exercise make a short line every time you have this worry again.

28
27
26
25
24
23
22
21
20
19
18
17
16
15
14
13
12
11
10
9
8
7
6
5
4
3
2
1

Worries

1 ....
....
....

2 ....
....
....

Week
3

3 ....
....
....

Day 17 Notes

1 Tick the boxes to indicate which subjects you have worried about today (you can give several answers).

studies/ work	finances	health	relationships	family/ friends	what others think of me	other
❏	❏	❏	❏	❏	❏	❏

2 Tick a box to indicate how many minutes/hours you have worried today.

0–30 minutes	30–60 minutes	1–2 hours	2–3 hours	3–4 hours	4–5 hours	> 5 hours
❏	❏	❏	❏	❏	❏	❏

3 Tick a box to indicate how much effort it took today to stop worrying, on a scale of 1 (almost no effort) to 5 (a great deal of effort).

no effort at all	almost no effort	some effort	quite a lot of effort	a great deal of effort
❏	❏	❏	❏	❏

4 How did you sleep last night? Indicate to what extent the following three statements apply to you.

	completely true	true	neutral	untrue	not true at all
I found it hard to get to sleep.	1	2	3	4	5
I suffered disturbed or broken sleep.	1	2	3	4	5
I awoke too early.	1	2	3	4	5

Week

3

5 **Event** Did anything particular happen today which made you start to worry? If so then write down what happened below, using key words.

....

....

....

....

....

....

....

....

....

Day 18 *Next worry*

Worry time I
Next please!
morning/afternoon

Explanation If you are troubled about something then you will be inclined to continually replay certain thought scenarios. The result is a constantly recurring stream of thoughts which feed one another. You can try the following technique to break this vicious circle (if possible use a kitchen timer).

a Begin with five minutes intense worrying.

b Now try to make a summary of your worries. Formulate each worry in detail, set the kitchen timer for one minute, concentrate for one minute on the first worry, then say to yourself, 'Next please!' and then continue with the next worry which is bothering you. After one minute, again say 'Next please!' to yourself. Continue with this until no more worries are left. Write down the content of each worry in several key words. It will surprise you how quickly you reach the point by which you can't think of any more worries.

Below write the key words for all 'Next please! thoughts'.

Next please!

28
27
26
25
24
23
22
21
20
19
18
17
16
15
14
13
12
11
10
9
8
7
6
5
4
3
2
1

Next please!

Next please!

Next please!

Next please!

In the meantime   If you begin to worry during the day, use the 'Next please!' method.

Worry time II
Gentle breathing exercises
evening

a   Begin with five minutes intense worrying.

b   Go and lie or sit in a comfortable position.

1   Shut your eyes and become aware of your breathing. Let your breathing continue at its natural rate.

2   Breathe in through your nose and out through your mouth. Breathe deeply from your abdomen. Put your hands on your stomach.

3   Concentrate on your breathing. You should find that focusing on your breathing makes you feel calm.

4   Begin to count. Every time you breathe in count one, and every time you breathe out count one. When you get to ten, start again.

5   You should notice that thoughts come into your head, thoughts about yesterday, about today and the future. Calmly let the thoughts be what they are, observe them, and then set them free. Observe them and then pay no more attention to them. Put the thoughts in little clouds and then let the clouds drift away.

6   Continue to concentrate on your breathing and on counting your breaths. If you get distracted then start counting your breaths again.

At night   Try putting your worries into your rucksack or shoebox under your bed where they will then stay until the next day. Then the following morning you can bring them out and look at them again.

28
27
26
25
24
23
22
21
20
19
18
17
16
15
14
13
12
11
10
9
8
7
6
5
4
3
2
1

Day 18 Notes

1   Tick the boxes to indicate which subjects you have worried about today (you can give several answers).

studies/ work	finances	health	relationships	family/ friends	what others think of me	other
❏	❏	❏	❏	❏	❏	❏

2   Tick a box to indicate how many minutes/hours you have worried today.

0–30 minutes	30–60 minutes	1–2 hours	2–3 hours	3–4 hours	4–5 hours	› 5 hours
❏	❏	❏	❏	❏	❏	❏

3   Tick a box to indicate how much effort it took today to stop worrying, on a scale of 1 (almost no effort) to 5 (a great deal of effort).

no effort at all	almost no effort	some effort	quite a lot of effort	a great deal of effort
❏	❏	❏	❏	❏

4 How did you sleep last night? Indicate to what extent the following three statements apply to you.

	completely true	true	neutral	untrue	not true at all
I found it hard to get to sleep.	1	2	3	4	5
I suffered disturbed or broken sleep.	1	2	3	4	5
I awoke too early.	1	2	3	4	5

5 **Event** Did anything particular happen today which made you start to worry? If so then write down what happened below, using key words.

....

....

....

....

....

....

....

....

....

....

Day 19 *Not now but later and looking at things*
        differently

Worry time I
Stop
morning/afternoon

Explanation The *not now but later* method is focused on worries
which, among other things, make it difficult to sleep. It is
useful for dealing with regularly recurring thoughts which are
irrational or disturbing. Sometimes they may make you
anxious, as with the recurring thought that someone is walking
around your house during the night.

Week

3

a   Begin with five minutes intense worrying.

b   We will now start the thought stop exercise. With your eyes
    closed you will express the constantly recurring thought in
    detail. During this account suddenly call out to yourself 'Not
    now but later' and postpone thinking this thought.

c   Repeat this five times.

In the meantime The thoughts will doubtless return and you can
    postpone them again using the procedure you have learned.
    You can perhaps intensify the effect by looking for some
    distraction after the *not now but later* technique.

Worry time II
Looking at things another way
evening

a Take a piece of paper and write down everything you like
about yourself. Don't stop until you have written at least three
things, the more the better.

b If you find this exercise difficult, then look at it from someone
else's point of view. How would your friends describe your
positive qualities? Once you have written down a number of
good points about yourself, then think about how you would
feel if at a party you were introduced to someone who had all
these positive qualities. There is a very good chance that you
will like this person, isn't there? Keep this sheet of paper with
you for a week and look at it several times a day to remind
yourself that you too have positive qualities. Look at it
whenever you start to worry.

At night   When undressing for bed, imagine that your clothes are
your worries. Take these off one after the other. Think about
your worries. With each piece of clothing you take off
consciously lay aside one worry.

28
27
26
25
24
23
22
21
20
19
18
17
16
15
14
13
12
11
10
9
8
7
6
5
4
3
2
1

Day 19 Notes

1   Tick the boxes to indicate which subjects you have worried
    about today (you can give several answers).

studies/ work	finances	health	relationships	family/ friends	what others think of me	other
❑	❑	❑	❑	❑	❑	❑

2   Tick a box to indicate how many minutes/hours you have
    worried today.

0–30 minutes	30–60 minutes	1–2 hours	2–3 hours	3–4 hours	4–5 hours	› 5 hours
❑	❑	❑	❑	❑	❑	❑

3   Tick a box to indicate how much effort it took today to stop
    worrying, on a scale of 1 (almost no effort) to 5 (a great deal
    of effort).

no effort at all	almost no effort	some effort	quite a lot of effort	a great deal of effort
❑	❑	❑	❑	❑

4 How did you sleep last night? Indicate to what extent the following three statements apply to you.

	completely true	true	neutral	untrue	not true at all
I found it hard to get to sleep.	1	2	3	4	5
I suffered disturbed or broken sleep.	1	2	3	4	5
I awoke too early.	1	2	3	4	5

5 **Event** Did anything particular happen today which made you start to worry? If so then write down what happened below, using key words.

....

....

....

....

....

....

....

....

....

28
27
26
25
24
23
22
21
20
19
18
17
16
15
14
13
12
11
10
9
8
7
6
5
4
3
2
1

Day 20 *Writing*

Worry time I
Writing exercise
morning/afternoon

a   Begin with five minutes intense worrying.

b   Get your pen and paper. Take an unpleasant incident from the past and think about it. Describe the event as fully as possible in the present tense as though it was happening now. Write down exactly what you are saying, and what the other person or people are saying. What are you thinking and feeling at the time? It is important to write down the details you remember about the situation, even if they do not seem relevant. For example, what you can smell, hear or see at the place it happened (colours, objects, sounds). What season is it? How is the weather?

In the meantime   If you worry in the meantime, you could consider trying one of the fantasy or relaxation exercises. Or if you are short of time, you could do the thought stop exercise again.

Week
3

Worry time II
Continuation of writing exercise
evening

a Begin with five minutes intense worrying.

b Now that you have described this event in the first worry time, write down what you found out about yourself in the situation. Then write down what you will do the next time in the same situation. Ask yourself to what extent the situation could have turned out differently, and how much control you really had over the situation. Try to accept the errors you made and to learn from them. Come to a conclusion for yourself. What have you learned? How can you ensure that the 'errors' you made don't happen again the next time? What could you do in the future?

c You have now finished this exercise, you cannot do anything more. You are now well prepared.

At night If you worry, change the phrase '*I must . . .*' into '*I want . . .*'

28
27
26
25
24
23
22
21
20
19
18
17
16
15
14
13
12
11
10
9
8
7
6
5
4
3
2
1

Day 20 Notes

1 Tick the boxes to indicate which subjects you have worried
about today (you can give several answers).

studies/ work	finances	health	relationships	family/ friends	what others think of me	other
❏	❏	❏	❏	❏	❏	❏

2 Tick a box to indicate how many minutes/hours you have
worried today.

0–30 minutes	30–60 minutes	1–2 hours	2–3 hours	3–4 hours	4–5 hours	> 5 hours
❏	❏	❏	❏	❏	❏	❏

3 Tick a box to indicate how much effort it took today to stop
worrying, on a scale of 1 (almost no effort) to 5 (a great deal
of effort).

no effort at all	almost no effort	some effort	quite a lot of effort	a great deal of effort
❏	❏	❏	❏	❏

4 How did you sleep last night? Indicate to what extent the following three statements apply to you.

	completely true	true	neutral	untrue	not true at all
I found it hard to get to sleep.	1	2	3	4	5
I suffered disturbed or broken sleep.	1	2	3	4	5
I awoke too early.	1	2	3	4	5

5 **Event** Did anything particular happen today which made you start to worry? If so then write down what happened below, using key words.

....

....

....

....

....

....

....

....

....

....

28
27
26
25
24
23
22
21
20
19
18
17
16
15
14
13
12
11
10
9
8
7
6
5
4
3
2
1

Day 21 *Relaxation*

Worry time 1
Whirling exercise
morning/afternoon

a   Begin with five minutes intense worrying.

b   Empty your mind for the following exercise. If thoughts come into your mind don't try to prevent this. Thoughts are just thoughts. Accept everything that comes to mind. Place these thoughts in light clouds. Let these clouds quietly whirl around in your head while you concentrate on your breathing. When you breathe out, you can quietly blow the clouds away. In this way you can allow the thoughts to come and then go again.

In the meantime   Try to do the talking in your imagination exercise (day 5). Or do the whirling exercise once more in the meantime.

Week

3

Worry time II

Relaxation

evening

a   Begin again with five minutes intense worrying.

b   Afterwards go and sit or lie as comfortably as possible in a
soft chair or on the bed.

1   Close your eyes and breathe deeply through your nose a
few times.
2   Feel your limbs become warm, heavy and relaxed.
3   Imagine that you are lying quietly on a warm beach or that
you are bobbing around in a boat.
4   Hold onto this image by thinking about the details, for
example, that you are enjoying the warm weather, it is not
too hot and not too cold. You are having a refreshing drink
and lying quietly.
5   Do this for five minutes.

At night   Imagine that you are having a fantastic time lying on the
beach. You are feeling really relaxed and enjoying feeling the
warmth of the sun's rays. Relax completely and feel your body
become heavier. Feel how your body is making an imprint in
the sand.

28
27
26
25
24
23
22
21
20
19
18
17
16
15
14
13
12
11
10
9
8
7
6
5
4
3
2
1

Day 21 Notes

1   Tick the boxes to indicate which subjects you have worried about today (you can give several answers).

studies/ work	finances	health	relationships	family/ friends	what others think of me	other
❏	❏	❏	❏	❏	❏	❏

2   Tick a box to indicate how many minutes/hours you have worried today.

0–30 minutes	30–60 minutes	1–2 hours	2–3 hours	3–4 hours	4–5 hours	› 5 hours
❏	❏	❏	❏	❏	❏	❏

3   Tick a box to indicate how much effort it took today to stop worrying, on a scale of 1 (almost no effort) to 5 (a great deal of effort).

no effort at all	almost no effort	some effort	quite a lot of effort	a great deal of effort
❏	❏	❏	❏	❏

4 How did you sleep last night? Indicate to what extent the following three statements apply to you.

	completely true	true	neutral	untrue	not true at all
I found it hard to get to sleep.	1	2	3	4	5
I suffered disturbed or broken sleep.	1	2	3	4	5
I awoke too early.	1	2	3	4	5

5 **Event** Did anything particular happen today which made you start to worry? If so then write down what happened below, using key words.

....

....

....

....

....

....

....

....

....

....

28
27
26
25
24
23
22
21
20
19
18
17
16
15
14
13
12
11
10
9
8
7
6
5
4
3
2
1

How much have you worried over the past week?

For each of the following statements indicate which is most applicable to you by circling the appropriate number. This applies to the past week.

		never	very rarely	rarely	some-times	often	very often	almost always
1	If I did not have enough time to do everything, I did not worry about it.	6	5	4	3	2	1	0
2	My worries overwhelmed me.	0	1	2	3	4	5	6
3	I didn't tend to worry about things.	6	5	4	3	2	1	0
4	Many situations made me worry.	0	1	2	3	4	5	6
5	I knew that I shouldn't have worried about things but I just couldn't help it.	0	1	2	3	4	5	6
6	When I was under pressure, I worried a lot.	0	1	2	3	4	5	6
7	I was always worrying about something.	0	1	2	3	4	5	6
8	I found it easy to dismiss worrisome thoughts.	6	5	4	3	2	1	0

	never	very rarely	rarely	some-times	often	very often	almost always
9 As soon as I finished one task, I started to worry about everything else that I had to do.	0	1	2	3	4	5	6
10 I did not worry about anything.	6	5	4	3	2	1	0
11 When there was nothing more I could do about a concern, I did not worry about it any more.	6	5	4	3	2	1	0
12 I noticed that I had been worrying about things.	0	1	2	3	4	5	6
13 Once I started worrying, I couldn't stop.	0	1	2	3	4	5	6
14 I worried all the time.	0	1	2	3	4	5	6
15 I worried about projects until they were all done.	0	1	2	3	4	5	6
Total							

▮▶ *Total score for the third week:*

28
27
26
25
24
23
22
21
20
19
18
17
16
15
14
13
12
11
10
9
8
7
6
5
4
3
2
1

Week
4

Day 22 *Three-column exercise*

Worry time I
Thinking habits
morning/afternoon

Explanation   On pages 114–15 there are three empty columns. The aim is to replace your negative thoughts with positive thoughts. On pages 112 and 113 there is an example of how to do the three-column exercise.

Step 1   Write down three worries in the first column.

Week

4

Step 2   Which thinking habits do you have with which worries? Choose from the following alternatives:

1   *Generalization*: Drawing general conclusions from a limited number of experiences.
2   Black and white thinking: You just think in extremes: something is always all good or all bad.
3   *Thought reading*: Assuming that you know exactly what other people are thinking in a certain situation.
4   *Limited perception*: You take a (negative) detail from a specific incident and focus your thoughts exclusively on this.
5   *Emotional thinking*: You take your feelings as proof for a certain thought being correct.
6   *Negative thinking*: With negative thinking you turn neutral or even positive experiences into negative ones.

In the meantime   Try to postpone worrying until the next worry time. If this does not work, look for some distraction or do one of the relaxation exercises. You could also choose to phone your chosen person X and tell them your worries.

Worry time II
Other habits
evening

Step 3   In the first worry time you have seen that some
thinking habits work against you. These thinking habits can be
changed into realistic ways of thinking. During this worry time
change all the worries from the first column into more realistic
thoughts. This means your task is this: complete column 3 with
more realistic thoughts.

At night   Try the exercise from yesterday night again. You are lying
on the beach. You are feeling incredibly relaxed and enjoying
feeling the warmth of the sun's rays. Relax completely and feel
your body become heavier. Feel how your body is making an
imprint in the sand.

28
27
26
25
24
23
22
21
20
19
18
17
16
15
14
13
12
11
10
9
8
7
6
5
4
3
2
1

Example of three-column exercise

Worry	Thinking habit	Realistic thought
Men can't be trusted	generalization	Some men can't be trusted but this is certainly not always the case
All they did was criticize me	limited perception	There was criticism but there were also other reactions
I feel stupid so I am stupid	emotional thinking	The fact that I feel inadequate in this situation does not mean that I am always inadequate
I can't do anything	black and white thinking	I can do some things better than others
They must be thinking: 'he's a right mug'	thought reading	I don't know what they think of me
She compliments me but she doesn't mean it	negative thinking and reading thoughts	Perhaps the compliment was genuine
If it's not right, then it must be wrong	black and white thinking	Most things are not 100% right or wrong
I never do anything good	generalization and limited perception	Some things go better for me than others. I am not perfect
If they don't think I'm nice then they must dislike me	black and white thinking	Other things are possible. I have my good points and bad points. Who doesn't?
He has decided he is going to make me look a fool	thought reading	I don't know what he is planning

Worry	Thinking habit	Realistic thought
They were not happy with the present, so they won't think it means anything	*black and white thinking and thought reading*	Perhaps it was not what they wanted. I can only ask them
Nothing goes well for me	*limited perception*	Sometimes things go well for me and sometimes not, the same as for everyone else

28
27
26
25
24
23
22
21
20
19
18
17
16
15
14
13
12
11
10
9
8
7
6
5
4
3
2
1

Step 1 *Worries*	Step 2 *Thinking Habits*

Step 3
Realistic thoughts

28

27

26

25

24

23

22

21

20

19

18

17

16

15

14

13

12

11

10

9

8

7

6

5

4

3

2

1

Day 22 Notes

1   Tick the boxes to indicate which subjects you have worried about today (you can give several answers).

studies/ work	finances	health	relationships	family/ friends	what others think of me	other
❏	❏	❏	❏	❏	❏	❏

2   Tick a box to indicate how many minutes/hours you have worried today.

0–30 minutes	30–60 minutes	1–2 hours	2–3 hours	3–4 hours	4–5 hours	› 5 hours
❏	❏	❏	❏	❏	❏	❏

3   Tick a box to indicate how much effort it took today to stop worrying, on a scale of 1 (almost no effort) to 5 (a great deal of effort).

no effort at all	almost no effort	some effort	quite a lot of effort	a great deal of effort
❏	❏	❏	❏	❏

Week

4

4 How did you sleep last night? Indicate to what extent the following three statements apply to you.

	completely true	true	neutral	untrue	not true at all
I found it hard to get to sleep.	1	2	3	4	5
I suffered disturbed or broken sleep.	1	2	3	4	5
I awoke too early.	1	2	3	4	5

5 **Event** Did anything particular happen today which made you start to worry? If so then write down what happened below, using key words.

....

....

....

....

....

....

....

....

....

....

28
27
26
25
24
23
22
21
20
19
18
17
16
15
14
13
12
11
10
9
8
7
6
5
4
3
2
1

Day 23 *Make a decision*

Worry time I
Make a decision
morning/afternoon

a Begin with five minutes intense worrying.

b **Explanation** Perhaps you will recognize this situation: You want to make a decision about something but you never do because you worry too much. You keep going round in circles about this decision, you are indecisive and this makes you passive. This results in the decision being postponed and you are stuck there worrying.

Week

4

You can use the following plan, which is in stages, to help you come to a decision. It is a good idea to write down your answers to the question, so that you have an overview and a plan. Get out some paper or a notebook and do the following exercise.

Step 1 What is the choice you have to make?
Example: Where should we go on holiday this year?

Step 2 What doubts do you have?
Example: Should we go to the same camping site as last year? Was it nice for the children? Shall we take the car on holiday or should we book an all-inclusive holiday? Won't that be far too expensive?

Step 3 Go and get some information to reduce your doubts. Options: A trip to the travel agent. Ask family and friends what they are going to do.

In the meantime   Step 4   Collect information (You can use the rest of the day to get this information, so that in the second worry time you can make a decision. Possible examples: Compare the different options such as price, play facilities for the children, for example. You can ask what is included in the price, what unforeseen expenses are to be expected. Ask other people how and where they are arranging their holidays.

Worry time II
Deadline
evening

Step 5   Weigh up the options against the information.

Step 6   Set a deadline. Decide for yourself how much time you want to spend on this decision. Do you want to think about it for another two weeks? Then set a deadline for two weeks time, note it in your diary, and make a decision within these two weeks.

Step 7   Evaluate your decision, not yourself.
   Every decision involves advantages and disadvantages and often you only get to know about them afterwards. It is not the case that there is only one right answer. A perfect decision does not exist, it is possible you will regret your decision later, but you can learn from this. It is possible that both alternatives are attractive and you have no regrets. Perhaps you can still cancel or change it. Also, you have taken a risk and life is not without its risks. Perhaps all the alternatives were equally as attractive or advantageous. It may also be the case that you are perfectly satisfied with your decision.

At night   If you start to worry, change the phrase: '*I must . . .*' into '*I want . . .*'

28
27
26
25
24
23
22
21
20
19
18
17
16
15
14
13
12
11
10
9
8
7
6
5
4
3
2
1

Day 23 Notes

1   Tick the boxes to indicate which subjects you have worried about today (you can give several answers).

studies/ work	finances	health	relationships	family/ friends	what others think of me	other
❏	❏	❏	❏	❏	❏	❏

2   Tick a box to indicate how many minutes/hours you have worried today.

0–30 minutes	30–60 minutes	1–2 hours	2–3 hours	3–4 hours	4–5 hours	› 5 hours
❏	❏	❏	❏	❏	❏	❏

3   Tick a box to indicate how much effort it took today to stop worrying, on a scale of 1 (almost no effort) to 5 (a great deal of effort).

no effort at all	almost no effort	some effort	quite a lot of effort	a great deal of effort
❏	❏	❏	❏	❏

4 How did you sleep last night? Indicate to what extent the following three statements apply to you.

	completely true	true	neutral	untrue	not true at all
I found it hard to get to sleep.	1	2	3	4	5
I suffered disturbed or broken sleep.	1	2	3	4	5
I awoke too early.	1	2	3	4	5

5 **Event** Did anything particular happen today which made you start to worry? If so then write down what happened below, using key words.

....

....

....

....

....

....

....

....

....

....

28
27
26
25
24
23
22
21
20
19
18
17
16
15
14
13
12
11
10
9
8
7
6
5
4
3
2
1

Day 24 *Looking forward*

Worry time I
Imagine that . . .
morning/afternoon

Week

4

Explanation   What life will be like within a certain period of time is a question which many people ask themselves. People can spend hours worrying about events they are very afraid of. This exercise is useful for people who are afraid that something bad is going to happen which they will not be able to cope with. At an earlier stage you wrote down some concerns in keywords on paper. We are now asking you to use one of your concerns for this exercise.

a   Begin with five minutes intense worrying.

b   Imagine what your life would be like if this concern became a reality tomorrow. The thing you are really afraid of is happening. Perhaps in the first instance this thought will be quite stressful in itself. But describe this situation in as much detail as possible. Whatever happens, describe it as though it is happening now. What are you feeling? What are your thoughts? In what sort of environment is this taking place? And what consequences does this have for you? Don't worry about spelling. Just write something.

   Example: 'I have not passed my exams, which I worked really hard for.' You very much blame yourself for this: 'I am not capable' or 'I am too stupid' or 'I am never going to finish this'. This is just one example of a negative event which can occur. How do you see your life in a year's time?

In the meantime   Read the exercise for the next worry time and think about it today.

Worry time II
What next?
evening

a   Begin with five minutes intense worrying.

b   Afterwards you are going to describe what your life will be like one year after the imaginary outcome of your worry. Imagine what your life will be like one year after the event you have feared. Describe how you feel one year later, and what your thoughts are. Try to think about the future logically: perhaps the future is bleak but this situation may not be insurmountable. New chances will have come up for you over this year. Write down too what pleasurable activities you could also have been involved in after this situation occurred. Your future is not a disaster but a situation which can be overcome.

At night   Try to postpone your worries until the next worry time. Use the distraction exercise, or positive worrying about a good memory you have or one of your good qualities.

Day 24 Notes

1   Tick the boxes to indicate which subjects you have worried about today (you can give several answers).

studies/ work	finances	health	relationships	family/ friends	what others think of me	other
❑	❑	❑	❑	❑	❑	❑

2   Tick a box to indicate how many minutes/hours you have worried today.

0–30 minutes	30–60 minutes	1–2 hours	2–3 hours	3–4 hours	4–5 hours	> 5 hours
❑	❑	❑	❑	❑	❑	❑

3   Tick a box to indicate how much effort it took today to stop worrying, on a scale of 1 (almost no effort) to 5 (a great deal of effort).

no effort at all	almost no effort	some effort	quite a lot of effort	a great deal of effort
❑	❑	❑	❑	❑

4 How did you sleep last night? Indicate to what extent the following three statements apply to you.

	completely true	true	neutral	untrue	not true at all
I found it hard to get to sleep.	1	2	3	4	5
I suffered disturbed or broken sleep.	1	2	3	4	5
I awoke too early.	1	2	3	4	5

5 **Event** Did anything particular happen today which made you start to worry? If so then write down what happened below, using key words.

....

....

....

....

....

....

....

....

....

....

Day 25 *Catch your thoughts*

Worry time I
Thought catching
morning/afternoon

a   Begin with five in minutes intense worrying.

b   Today every time you have a worry, say it out loud to yourself. Before saying the worry, put the words 'I think' in front of it. For example, 'I think that I don't spend enough time with my children and I am perhaps too busy with my career.' Note these thoughts down on a sheet of paper. Do this straightaway as otherwise you may forget them. Note the situation in which these thoughts occurred. Also note how upsetting you found them on a scale of 0 to 10.

In the meantime   When you worry, imagine you are on a short holiday. For half an hour let yourself enjoy that lovely, carefree holiday feeling. Do something nice, buy a newspaper, for example, and enjoy a half-hour holiday.

Week

4

Worry time II
Putting your thoughts in context
evening

a   Begin with five minutes intense worrying.

b   In this worry time we are going to take a closer look at the
thoughts you have had today. Choose the thought which has
occurred most frequently or which you have found the most
upsetting. Answer the following questions on paper or in your
notebook:

1   What does this thought say about me?
2   What does this thought say about my world, my friends
and my family?
3   What is the worst thing about this situation, these
thoughts and this feeling? Why is it so bad?
4   What is it that makes the thought so distracting and why
do I find it so troubling?

At night   Imagine that you are once again having a fantastic time
lying on the beach. You are feeling really relaxed and enjoying
feeling the warmth of the sun's rays. Relax completely and feel
your body become heavier. Feel how your body is making an
imprint in the sand.

28
27
26
25
24
23
22
21
20
19
18
17
16
15
14
13
12
11
10
9
8
7
6
5
4
3
2
1

Day 25 Notes

1   Tick the boxes to indicate which subjects you have worried
    about today (you can give several answers).

studies/ work	finances	health	relationships	family/ friends	what others think of me	other
❏	❏	❏	❏	❏	❏	❏

2   Tick a box to indicate how many minutes/hours you have
    worried today.

0–30 minutes	30–60 minutes	1–2 hours	2–3 hours	3–4 hours	4–5 hours	› 5 hours
❏	❏	❏	❏	❏	❏	❏

3   Tick a box to indicate how much effort it took today to stop
    worrying, on a scale of 1 (almost no effort) to 5 (a great deal
    of effort).

no effort at all	almost no effort	some effort	quite a lot of effort	a great deal of effort
❏	❏	❏	❏	❏

Week

4

4 How did you sleep last night? Indicate to what extent the following three statements apply to you.

	completely true	true	neutral	untrue	not true at all
I found it hard to get to sleep.	1	2	3	4	5
I suffered disturbed or broken sleep.	1	2	3	4	5
I awoke too early.	1	2	3	4	5

5 **Event** Did anything particular happen today which made you start to worry? If so then write down what happened below, using key words.

....

....

....

....

....

....

....

....

....

28
27
26
25
24
23
22
21
20
19
18
17
16
15
14
13
12
11
10
9
8
7
6
5
4
3
2
1

Day 26 *A realistic approach*

Worry time I
A realistic approach
morning/afternoon

Explanation   In the exercise we are going to look for realistic thoughts. The thought pattern you have fallen into cannot be unlearned all at once. Every time you must replace your thoughts with realistic thoughts. It will be a while before this becomes second nature. Take your time.

Week

4

   Answer the questions below, using the results from the three-column exercise.

a   Begin with five minutes intense worrying.

b1 Describe the problem:
   What is worrying you? Describe the situation.
   In what direction are your thoughts taking you?
   Where do things go wrong?
   What is the underlying need/disaster/theme of your thoughts?

b2 Give evidence for your worries:
   What evidence is there for the validity of your worries?
   What evidence is there for the non-validity of your worries?

b3 State your aims:
   What would you like to be different and better? Think about this and give your imagination free rein.

b4 Think of realistic alternatives:
   What is the worst that can happen?
   What would be the most positive solution for you?
   What would be the most realistic solution?

In the meantime   Try the talking in your imagination exercise from
day 5 again. You could also telephone someone and tell them
your worries. Make sure they don't react but just listen.

Worry time II
A realistic approach (continuation)
evening

b5   Look at the following consequences:
Imagine that you are going to actually put the most realistic
solution of b4 into practice and think about what it will mean
for you.
What are the positive and negative consequences of this
solution in the short and the long term?

b6   Put this new realistic approach into practice:
Make it a habit to have a realistic outlook. Act in accordance
with this realistic outlook.

b7   Assess the results, give yourself the time to take ownership of
these new realistic thoughts. After a while you will see that
this will become automatic.

At night   Try the muscle relaxation exercise once more when you
are in bed.

28
27
26
25
24
23
22
21
20
19
18
17
16
15
14
13
12
11
10
9
8
7
6
5
4
3
2
1

Day 26 Notes

1   Tick the boxes to indicate which subjects you have worried
about today (you can give several answers).

studies/ work	finances	health	relationships	family/ friends	what others think of me	other
❏	❏	❏	❏	❏	❏	❏

Week

4

2   Tick a box to indicate how many minutes/hours you have
worried today.

0–30 minutes	30–60 minutes	1–2 hours	2–3 hours	3–4 hours	4–5 hours	› 5 hours
❏	❏	❏	❏	❏	❏	❏

3   Tick a box to indicate how much effort it took today to stop
worrying, on a scale of 1 (almost no effort) to 5 (a great deal
of effort).

no effort at all	almost no effort	some effort	quite a lot of effort	a great deal of effort
❏	❏	❏	❏	❏

4 How did you sleep last night? Indicate to what extent the
following three statements apply to you.

	completely true	true	neutral	untrue	not true at all
I found it hard to get to sleep.	1	2	3	4	5
I suffered disturbed or broken sleep.	1	2	3	4	5
I awoke too early.	1	2	3	4	5

5 **Event** Did anything particular happen today which made you
start to worry? If so then write down what happened below,
using key words.

....

....

....

....

....

....

....

....

....

....

Day 27 *Free choice*

Worry time I
Choose for yourself
morning/afternoon

a Begin with five minutes intense worrying.

b You have done a lot of exercises over the past few weeks. You will have found some exercises more beneficial/useful to do than others. This is why we are going to let you choose for yourself which exercise you want to do today.

Now choose the exercise from the first two weeks from which you feel you have benefitted the most, and do this now.

In the meantime Try to postpone your worries until the next worry time. If that does not work, do the positive worrying 1 exercise about a good memory you have or positive worrying 2 exercise about one of your good qualities.

Week
4

Worry time II
Choose for yourself
evening

a Begin with five minutes intense worrying.

b Now choose the exercise from the last two weeks from which
you feel you have benefitted the most, and do this now.

At night If you are worrying about what you have got planned
change the phrase: '*I must . . .*' into '*I want . . .*'

Day 27 Notes

1   Tick the boxes to indicate which subjects you have worried
    about today (you can give several answers).

studies/ work	finances	health	relationships	family/ friends	what others think of me	other
❑	❑	❑	❑	❑	❑	❑

Week

4

2   Tick a box to indicate how many minutes/hours you have
    worried today.

0–30 minutes	30–60 minutes	1–2 hours	2–3 hours	3–4 hours	4–5 hours	› 5 hours
❑	❑	❑	❑	❑	❑	❑

3   Tick a box to indicate how much effort it took today to stop
    worrying, on a scale of 1 (almost no effort) to 5 (a great deal
    of effort).

no effort at all	almost no effort	some effort	quite a lot of effort	a great deal of effort
❑	❑	❑	❑	❑

4 How did you sleep last night? Indicate to what extent the following three statements apply to you.

	completely true	true	neutral	untrue	not true at all
I found it hard to get to sleep.	1	2	3	4	5
I suffered disturbed or broken sleep.	1	2	3	4	5
I awoke too early.	1	2	3	4	5

5 **Event** Did anything particular happen today which made you start to worry? If so then write down what happened below, using key words.

....

....

....

....

....

....

....

....

....

....

28
27
26
25
24
23
22
21
20
19
18
17
16
15
14
13
12
11
10
9
8
7
6
5
4
3
2
1

Day 28 *A positive day*

Worry time I
Positive thinking exercise
morning/afternoon

a Begin with five minutes intense worrying.

b Go and sit down quietly. Acknowledge your anxiety and your worries, gather them up and let them be. Now you are not going to concentrate on the things you are dissatisfied with or which you worry about but on something you are proud of. Shut your eyes. Take time to let something come to mind, a positive quality, a special achievement, something which makes you proud of yourself, something you have done.

When you have found this quality, think about your achievement and then tell (yourself) quietly in one sentence that you are proud of yourself.

.... (your name) **when you** .... you did a fantastic job, I am proud of you!

.... (your name) **your** .... is a great quality you have, I am proud of you!

Then repeat this phrase ten times in your head and say it in your mind with ever increasing conviction and enthusiasm. Finally you can even shout it out (in your mind). In this way you will see that positive thoughts have a strength which will make you feel good again. Accept that you have good qualities as well as bad qualities, the same as everyone else.

In the meantime There is an exercise which you can do again in the meantime if you start to worry: clap your hands and say to yourself, 'Not now but later!' You could also even take a half-hour holiday.

Worry time II
Positive worrying
evening

a Begin with five minutes intense worrying.

b Write a positive account of yourself but try to be realistic. Write about your personality, your good and bad points, your life and your future. Write about what is important to you. Are these things achievable? What are your wishes for the coming weeks or months? Are they realistic, are they also what you really want and not influenced by others? Set targets which are as small as possible. Are you on your way to achieving your goal? If not, then you must put this goal to one side and make your goals attainable.

At night If you worry, do the thought whirling exercise.

Day 28 Notes

1   Tick the boxes to indicate which subjects you have worried about today (you can give several answers).

studies/ work	finances	health	relationships	family/ friends	what others think of me	other
❑	❑	❑	❑	❑	❑	❑

2   Tick a box to indicate how many minutes/hours you have worried today.

0–30 minutes	30–60 minutes	1–2 hours	2–3 hours	3–4 hours	4–5 hours	› 5 hours
❑	❑	❑	❑	❑	❑	❑

3   Tick a box to indicate how much effort it took today to stop worrying, on a scale of 1 (almost no effort) to 5 (a great deal of effort).

no effort at all	almost no effort	some effort	quite a lot of effort	a great deal of effort
❑	❑	❑	❑	❑

4   How did you sleep last night? Indicate to what extent the following three statements apply to you.

	completely true	true	neutral	untrue	not true at all
I found it hard to get to sleep.	1	2	3	4	5
I suffered disturbed or broken sleep.	1	2	3	4	5
I awoke too early.	1	2	3	4	5

5   **Event**   Did anything particular happen today which made you start to worry? If so then write down what happened below, using key words.

....

....

....

....

....

....

....

....

....

28
27
26
25
24
23
22
21
20
19
18
17
16
15
14
13
12
11
10
9
8
7
6
5
4
3
2
1

How much have you worried over the past week?

For each of the following statements indicate which is most applicable to you by circling the appropriate number. This applies to the past week.

Week

4

		never	very rarely	rarely	some-times	often	very often	almost always
1	If I did not have enough time to do everything, I did not worry about it.	6	5	4	3	2	1	0
2	My worries overwhelmed me.	0	1	2	3	4	5	6
3	I didn't tend to worry about things.	6	5	4	3	2	1	0
4	Many situations made me worry.	0	1	2	3	4	5	6
5	I knew that I shouldn't have worried about things but I just couldn't help it.	0	1	2	3	4	5	6
6	When I was under pressure, I worried a lot.	0	1	2	3	4	5	6
7	I was always worrying about something.	0	1	2	3	4	5	6
8	I found it easy to dismiss worrisome thoughts.	6	5	4	3	2	1	0

	never	very rarely	rarely	some-times	often	very often	almost always
9 As soon as I finished one task, I started to worry about everything else that I had to do.	0	1	2	3	4	5	6
10 I did not worry about anything.	6	5	4	3	2	1	0
11 When there was nothing more I could do about a concern, I did not worry about it any more.	6	5	4	3	2	1	0
12 I noticed that I had been worrying about things.	0	1	2	3	4	5	6
13 Once I started worrying, I couldn't stop.	0	1	2	3	4	5	6
14 I worried all the time.	0	1	2	3	4	5	6
15 I worried about projects until they were all done.	0	1	2	3	4	5	6
Total							

➠ *Total score for the fourth week:*

End of Part 1

The aim of this book is to teach you how to reduce your worrying and how to have more control over your thoughts. You have learned a number of exercises to help you to do this. If by doing the exercises you have succeeded in reducing your worrying, then it is advisable to continue with them. It is best for you to decide for yourself which exercises you want to continue with and which exercises you have found most helpful in achieving this.

Week

4

Worriers do not let go of their worrying thoughts easily and this is because they are anxious that they will lose control of a problem. They feel that they are solving the problem with this way of thinking. Up to a point that may be so, if you do find a solution or end up taking action, but excessive worrying will not solve your problems. It is important that you realize this.

Positive emotions broaden our outlook on things and make us more creative when thinking about solutions to our problems. It is important in our daily lives that we regularly create situations in which we have the possibility of experiencing positive emotions. These can take any form as long as they make you feel good. Meditation, for example, or a walk in the wood, a hobby, drinking a cup of coffee, etc. Don't wait until you start worrying again because then it is often difficult for that reason to motivate yourself to go and do anything. The advice is to use positive emotions on a daily basis. Just the fact that you regularly do something which is good for you can help you to feel better. This in turn will increase your feeling of being in control.

How much less am I worrying now?

In the following table you can note down your total scores from the worry questionnaires that you completed at the end of each week. This will give you an insight into the progress you have made with your behaviour in terms of worrying. Are you worrying less now?

	Score
Total score on the worry list at the beginning	
Total score on the worry list at the end of week 1	
Total score on the worry list at the end of week 2	
Total score on the worry list at the end of week 3	
Total score on the worry list at the end of week 4	

If your score on the last worry list is less than half that of the score you had at the beginning, then we congratulate you on the result you have achieved. If your score is between 25 and 50 per cent lower than it was at the beginning, then we advise that you continue with the exercises. If your score is a reduction of less than 25 per cent or it has remained the same or it has even increased, then it would be advisable for you to discuss with your GP whether treatment with a psychologist, psychotherapist or psychiatrist is necessary. It is not advisable to wait too long before seeking professional help because excessive worrying will not, in the majority of cases, decrease by itself.

Part 2

Worrying for advanced students

Some worries are very persistent. This is because in the majority of cases we don't notice these worries creeping up on us. Then we grow so accustomed to these self-invented 'cobwebs' blowing around our heads that we don't notice them. These thoughts have become automatic. Sometimes we believe our own little fabrication to be the truth. Sometimes we exaggerate. Our own thoughts often make us suffer a great deal. The inability to sleep is the best indication that we are worrying (although the inability to sleep is not always necessarily an indication of worrying).

Worries have the habit of making their existence obvious. 'You see I'm stupid, you see I can't do anything, you see that I'm not good enough, that I can't get my words out etc. etc.' For convenience we will refer to this as the 'you seeism-complex'. If you practise this a lot, then you are always right. Except you are not really right, because in the majority of cases it is simply not true.

What is difficult is that many thoughts taken in isolation do not have to become worries but they become worries when memorized by constant repetition. If someone moves from the city centre into a house in a newly built suburb and complains that 'I feel as though I am buried alive here', by which he means that he doesn't have many visitors and he misses the former sense of social cohesion, then there is nothing wrong in expressing this. It is a metaphor with a slight degree of exaggeration. However, if some weeks later this phrase still continuously crops up in a person's thoughts (that is to say, several dozen times a day), then we are dealing with a worry.

The difference between normal thoughts and worries lies mainly in their high frequency, duration and our lack of control over them. Thoughts about a problem which go through one's head for several days and which result in a decision are not worries. Thoughts about a problem which occupy you for several weeks without a solution then being found probably are worries. A feature of worries is that they always come back, including at times when you don't want them to, and no solution or decision follows, nor

any relief, which leads to fatigue. Worries often cause emotional exhaustion due to the lack of sleep and hopelessness which eventually results. You feel as though you are being kicked around like a football by your uncontrollable thoughts.

Another feature of worrying is that it takes up a great deal of time. Real worriers can all too easily spend many hours a day thinking of nothing other than their worries. We should not brush this aside lightly. People who worry can sometimes lose ten hours a day on their worries. And some will spend fifteen hours a day or more worrying. Some people claim to spend all their waking hours worrying and there are even people who claim that they lie worrying during the night in their sleep and in their dreams. Research in the meantime has shown that the brain activity that takes place during worrying also usually continues in some people when they are asleep.

Another feature of the worrying of those who do it persistently is that in the majority of cases they worry about a limited number of subjects. In most cases they worry about one or two subjects and in some cases three. But the subjects themselves are endlessly repeated in many variations.

This part is especially intended for people who are persistent worriers. Some commonly occurring worries are dealt with in stages and a commentary is provided. Possible alternatives for these worries are given. You may notice that you easily recognize the worries other people have, but that it is difficult to recognize your own worries. This is just the way we are made as people. You can easily see how little sense there is in some of the worries other people have and you may think yourself lucky that you do not share these worries. Your own worries, however, seem sensible and necessary. This book will help you to question the logic of some of your favourite worries.

In this book you have already learned how to spot, write down and challenge your worries. In this part we are going to go further with these persistent worries. We will look at their content but we will also take the form of the worry, into consideration

such as frequency, intensity, duration, repetition, degree of reality, etc.

After some time you may notice that exactly what you are worrying about is really not that important. It is much more important to notice that you are worrying and that this is not getting you anywhere. You waste a lot of time worrying. And it does not solve your problems in any way. As soon as you realize this, you can start to blow these webs of worry away.

For some people worrying is closely linked with their level of anxiety and depression. Even when that is the case, by tackling your worrying you can to some degree reduce your level of anxiety or depression. It is important that you do not set your hopes too high, but this applies to all other readers too.

Some persistent worriers feel so powerless in the face of their own thoughts that they just don't want to think any longer. Sometimes people take too many pills or drink too much alcohol so as to blot out their thoughts, stop them or eliminate them entirely. Some people experience suicidal thoughts as a result of endless worrying. Suicidal thoughts therefore can be regarded as an extreme form of worrying. This book is also intended for readers who sometimes just want to stop these thoughts altogether.

Favourite worries

1 I am not good enough

Perhaps the most popular worry is: 'I am not good enough.' If you think or say this repeatedly then you will probably end up being trapped in very frequent fits of worry. Now you might imagine that you lack self-confidence and that this is why you end up saying these things. But perhaps it would be better to view the sequence in another way, that is to say, if you keep on saying this type of thing then you will end up lacking confidence. Or you will end up believing that you are not a good mother, or that you have

shortcomings as a husband or wife, or as a teacher or that you cannot do DIY properly. These statements are made in the spirit of all or nothing. The whole person is degraded and not just what has been achieved. A significant feature of these and similar thoughts is that they can become self-fulfilling, that is to say that if you think you are not good enough, then you are going to behave accordingly like a man or a woman who is insecure about themselves, and there will be a good chance that this will lead to a reduced level of achievement, which means that you will have more reason to think of yourself as not good enough (you see). In the end, others will see this too. This is what is referred to as a self-fulfilling prophecy, a prophecy that becomes true on its own. This is a recurring feature of many worries.

The challenge

What is striking is that worriers accept the statement: 'I am not good enough' as the truth without stopping to examine how much truth there really is in this statement. Because what does 'not good enough' really mean? Many worriers set themselves very high standards. Sometimes they are too perfectionist. And if they only fulfil 90 per cent of their own requirements they feel they have not performed adequately. Compare this with the high jumper who has set himself the target of being able to jump 2 metres in height. After many years training he can only just clear 1.98 metres. He might think that he had at least almost achieved his target. In that case he would not be a worrier. A real worrier would view this achievement as not good enough. And perhaps not just his performance but possibly also his whole person. Because he maintains that he should have trained harder, should have been more ambitious, been a stronger character, etc. And so the maximum achievement is devalued in the eyes of a worrier to an achievement which was not good enough, performed by an athlete who was not good enough as a person. But what is 'good' really? Even the term 'good' is rather vague. What does one understand by a 'good' mother, a 'good' spouse, a 'good' researcher?

The evaluation of behaviour fitting to the role of mothers, spouses or researchers does not have much to do with the term 'good'. Much more specific qualifications are required for these, which are themselves also somewhat subjective. In short, the term 'good' is almost always a subjective standard, and everyone understands something different by it. And why should you want to go along with what someone else finds good? What is important is that you should first clearly define your own norms and standards of performance. And when things do not go well, it therefore makes no sense to ask yourself whether or not you can measure up to unclear criteria. Moreover, if you want to be perfect as a mother then your children will probably have no life.

Alternative

It is important, if you feel the need for this, to create a suitable alternative for yourself (and write this down). An alternative for this phrase could be: 'I have many roles and do many activities, and in the case of each of these roles I can ask myself whether I may want to grow further. If I enjoy cooking then I can get more training, or I can take courses in DIY, and in my role as a mother I can ask for tips from other mothers, etc. Let me try to be a normal housewife and mother, a good-enough mother, a mother who does what she likes to do with the children' (and the same for fathers or people who want to do DIY). An alternative for people who go out to work could be: 'If I assume that I am not yet fulfilling the requirements of my employer in terms of my work then I can get more qualifications. Let me use my superior's judgement rather than judging myself initially.'

2 Nobody likes me

This is a popular worry. This worry too can be self-fulfilling: If you think this for long enough and you believe it, then this statement will to a certain extent become true, because you will behave like

an insecure person who is wanting to be liked but who is not always liked (you see).

Watch out for the all or nothing attitude. Nobody likes me, that is to say there is not one person who likes me. The meaning of this thought is of course also the conviction that my personality is so bad that nobody can like me. And that all social situations will end in the same way: with rejection.

The challenge

This statement is, in general, not true. If you believe this statement to be true, then you have not grasped the fact that in reality you are liked, just not by everyone, and not by everyone whom you would want to like you. If you repeat a statement of this kind to yourself, then you will become reconciled to the problem of getting people to like you. And then you will be very different indeed to people who set little store by the judgements of others. In short, people who fear rejection often come across as very likeable when you encounter them in everyday life. It is just that in the long term people can sometimes get tired of the exaggerated friendliness with which these worriers pester the people they know. You may also interpret all clear signs of liking or warmth around you incorrectly: 'They are just saying they like me but really they think I'm nothing', thus not believing the reassurances to the contrary.

Also being liked is not everything. This is because there are several ways in which we can be liked. These may be a superficial first impression or a substantial impression which has been built up over several years. The first impression is important if a good second impression follows on from it. Some charmers can make an excellent first impression only to then use this charm to swindle people. Some very likeable people turn out to be tyrants in their private lives and some grumpy people who do not seem very likeable can turn out in private to be extraordinarily helpful and deserving. When people like you, in the majority of cases this is because your behaviour or appearance is of help to them, or makes them think of someone dear to them. Your behaviour suits their

agenda. In short; to be liked is something which is just registered momentarily, and does not say everything about you by a long way. It is better if you can focus on people you like yourself. And then just wait to see if the feeling is mutual.

Alternative

If you have these types of thoughts frequently then perhaps think about the following statement (you can write your own alternative in a notebook): 'There is no single person in the world who is liked by everyone (except for some film stars but they have no life). There are some people who have great social skills and who are liked by many people. There are a lot of people who have quite normal skills in terms of how they interact with others and who are liked by some people but not by others. This is because everyone has their good and bad points and sometimes that says more about other people than about me. It is just a matter of chance whether I am liked and by whom I am liked. In addition, people can make of me what they will – I don't have much influence over that. However nice I am is no guarantee that the people will like me. It is much more important for me to like other people. If I take stock of who I like and focus on them, then I increase the chance that the positive impression is mutual.'

3 I can't do that

This thought may be true. For example, you cannot fly, therefore you can't do that. But people often use this statement both appropriately and inappropriately. In particular if you repeat it often then it can turn into a worry which will mean that you do not start to do the things you really want to do. 'That is too difficult for me' is a variant of this. Or 'I won't succeed in doing that'. Remember that we are dealing with predictions here: 'If I tackle this or that then I won't succeed at it, that is too difficult for me, or it will turn out that I can't do it.' Success is excluded in advance. Then you are going to end up looking for obstacles everywhere

and you will end up not doing the difficult task. 'I wouldn't dare do that' is a statement from the same category.

The challenge

Again, sometimes this prediction may be correct but in many cases it won't. Take, for example, changing a burst tyre on a car or a punctured tyre on a bike. Some people will say immediately that they can't do this but what they really mean is that they don't know how to do it at present. But with some explanations and practice, it should be the case that practically every person can learn to repair a puncture on a bike or how to replace a burst tyre. Or when someone asks you to make a short speech at the wedding of a good friend. You then react straightaway by saying 'I can't do that' and you always do this whenever anyone asks you to do anything difficult – this can then turn into a worry, which here too will once again end up coming true. Because if you always think or say: 'I can't do that' then in the long term, you will end up not learning very much. What many people also mean when they say; 'I can't do that' is: 'That is really difficult.' But often if you just try something you will end up succeeding. It is therefore better to think: 'That is difficult but not impossible.' This is because most things can be learned. If you don't know how to replace a water tap, or how to change a spark plug, or how to commence legal proceedings to fight a ruling concerning seeing the children after a divorce, then it does not help to say that you can't do this. You can always start by asking for some information or help first, and then it may well turn out that the task in question is not beyond your capabilities.

It always helps to look at the word *that* from the statement 'I can't do that' a little more closely and to break it down. Because if the word *that* stands for fitting a radiator, then this task can be broken down as follows: [1] look for information in books or on the Internet; [2] ask a friend with practical skills how it should be done; [3] look into what materials you will need; [4] look into what tools you will need; [5] check how expensive it would be to pay a

professional; [6] see if a friend with practical skills would support you; [7] follow a course in fitting radiators at a local college of further education, and [8] check how much time and money you have available. In the time that you will have spent taking these steps the fitting of the radiator has come a little closer.

In short, some things are difficult but not impossible.

Alternative

Always try to make it clear what you mean by *that* (cook a tasty meal? Write a letter?) and bear in mind that 'perhaps some things are difficult and at present you do not have sufficient knowledge and skills, but that many things can be learned and many things can be achieved by taking them one step at a time'. In brief: 'It is difficult but not impossible.' The suggestion here is that every time you find yourself trapped by the thought: 'I can't do that' replace this thought with: 'I don't know if I can do that yet, I shall go and learn how to do it first and then try it.' The statement: 'That is too difficult for me' could be replaced by: 'That is too difficult for me now but if I want to learn about it then I can go and start on it'. The statement: 'I wouldn't dare' can be replaced by: 'I do find it a bit scary but perhaps I could be daring and do it if I am well-prepared.'

4 I won't be able to cope

'I won't be able to cope' is the expression people use when they imagine a future event which is bound to be linked with negative emotions. For example, if you have a fear of flying and you are planning to travel by plane then this could prompt you to think about the unbearable panic you might experience. Or you might anticipate a moment of panic when you have to get in a lift and you are afraid of lifts. Equally, you might be afraid of going through life alone after a divorce. If you regularly think: 'I won't be able to cope' then that can lead to a suffocating attitude to life built around avoidance, which is based on nothing other than

continuous worrying about the intolerable anxiety which you believe you will feel in the future. That means you are feeling anxious about future anxiety.

The challenge

To be precise, what you are afraid of is your own intolerable anxiety which you think you will suffer when something bad happens. You are afraid of not being able to tolerate the panic you will feel in the future, the distress, the loneliness. In reality most people (and probably you too) can cope quite adequately with anxiety, distress, loneliness, dejection, etc. If next week you get into a panic when you faint in a crowded shop, then this type of panic can be tolerated quite well. If you let the feeling of panic pass and you just wait half an hour, then the panic will in the majority of cases subside and you will in fact have survived the panic attack. In fact nothing happened, you just had a panic attack which is of course inconvenient but not disastrous. In reality you are not going to have a heart attack, nor will your hair suddenly turn grey, your loved ones will not leave you in the lurch and bystanders will, for the most part, offer well-meaning sympathy. In short, almost everyone will survive a panic attack. That does not mean it is pleasant but in reality you will be able to cope with it. You too can cope with feelings of anxiety.

The problem is that if you try to escape the panic then the avoidance tactics often cause more damage than the anxiety itself. Take the following case. A woman was in her car on the way to work when she saw a small spider hanging from her rear view mirror. Because she was afraid of spiders she tried to kill it by hitting it with a newspaper but in so doing she ended up crashing her car into a lamppost. The moral of the story: it is much better to accept your anxiety than to use all these avoidance tactics. Then there was a man who was so anxious about losing his partner to another man that he panicked about it and then spied on his wife to such an extent that she did in fact end up leaving him. In short: expressing your anxiety is often less harmful than all those

attempts to escape it. Moreover, escaping your anxiety does not work: the more frequently you run away from your anxiety the stronger these feelings will become.

The best remedy is to accept your feelings of anxiety, to tolerate them and not try to escape them. Then these feelings of anxiety will die down.

Alternative

Why not try one of the following phrases?: 'If I feel anxious or get into a panic, then I will be able to cope.' 'It is just inconvenient but I don't need to run away from my anxieties.' 'If I do end up on my own after the divorce, then I will be able to cope with that in the end. It will be very difficult but I will survive it.' 'When I am scared by my anxiety, then I will go and sit down quietly and wait until the anxiety passes.' 'I accept that I am scared and I will wait until the anxiety just dies down.'

5 I am stupid

The statement 'I am stupid' and similar statements such as: 'I don't know a lot, other people know a lot more, I can't remember anything, they'll think I am really stupid', etc. are very common.

People who say these things about themselves lack self-confidence and are perhaps beginning to suffer from depression. That is the best way to make yourself feel useless. It is also a good example of the you seeism complex: 'You see, my husband always knows much more about everything.' It is incredible that some people carry on saying these things against themselves for decades and then end up believing them to be true.

The challenge

It is striking that people who think of themselves as stupid often do not know exactly what they mean by the term 'stupid'. When asked they struggle to give a definition of or criteria for what they understand by the terms 'stupid'. Because 'stupid' is not the same as

not intelligent. There are plenty of intelligent people (because they have done A levels or gone to college or university) who call themselves stupid. And even people with a low IQ or with a mental handicap are not stupid, just limited in their abilities.

Stupid is a term which is used to indicate that someone should have known better, should have given something more consideration, or someone who has done something stupid through laziness or thoughtlessness. Stupidity is thus a subjective judgement at the core of which is the idea that you could have done something better if you had thought about it more. But worriers don't use or no longer use the term in that sense. They objectively believe that for once and for all they are completely unintelligent.

Alternative

Try to write an alternative definition for this thought in your notebook or use one of the following phrases: 'I do make mistakes now and again just like everyone does, and from time to time it happens that when I think about a situation I realize I should have thought harder about it, but I am not stupid. Everyone sometimes has thought processes which are not very clever but that doesn't mean I am not intelligent. I am usually as clever as most people with my level of education, and sometimes even more clever and sometimes not as clever. And even if I have a low IQ (which has not yet been proven), I can't do anything about it and I should not get upset about it.'

6 I don't know what I want

It is not rare for worriers to tell themselves they do not know what they want. And then they say this as though it was self-evident. Real worriers have said this to themselves so many times that their whole lives are lived on this basis. The effect is that people become crippled by their inability to make choices, and they end up becoming passive and apathetic. This statement often goes

together with: 'I can't choose.' And even more extreme: the statement about not knowing what you want is used as an explanation for the feeling that you are unable to make a choice. Some people can no longer even choose between tomato and vegetable soup in a restaurant, at which point they then decide to eliminate the need to make such a choice for ever by not going out for a meal again.

The challenge

In general, this statement is not true at all. Worriers often know what they want, but they don't dare to voice this, or they have wishes and preferences but they think they don't have good enough arguments for these preferences. If you question them more closely, worriers have the same preferences (for example music, holiday destinations) as other people but when it comes to important decisions they act as though they do not want to trust in their own preferences. First of all, what may be referred to as an in-depth analysis has to be carried out of all the pros and cons before you are able to make a choice. But of course decisions are not made like that. The best decisions are not those where you have thought about it extensively overnight but the decisions where you go with your (spontaneous) preference. Moreover, if you do make a wrong decision then you can always go back on it or change it at a later stage. And if you can choose between attractive alternatives then you can never make the wrong decision.

Alternative

Just try one of the following statements: 'Mostly I know what I like and what I don't like, and usually I succeed in making a decision I am happy with. But sometimes it is hard to choose. I try as hard as I can to take my own advice about what I have up to now found really always suits me best. This means I don't have to over-analyse. I may usually do and have what I like.' 'My life does not depend on which choice I make. Perhaps later it will turn out that the chosen alternative was not the best one but then a little

bad luck is normal. I'll just let myself make a choice, by tossing a coin if I have to, and just see what happens.'

7 I am a failure

If you say this to yourself ten times a day, then in the end you will start to think really negatively about yourself. The following are in the same category: 'I have never succeeded at anything' or 'Nothing ever works out for me' Or 'I've never finished anything well'. Note how generalized this judgement is: a failure. Sometime people even add to this: a *complete* failure.

The challenge

This is a good example of 'all or nothing' thinking: 'If I did not succeed in doing what I wanted to, then that means I am a complete failure. It does not matter if anything did get finished or achieved, the required standard was not good enough and I am therefore a complete failure.' Persistent worriers believe this completely and regard it as the truth. Less persistent worriers know that this is nonsense but in spite of this they cannot get the thought out of their head and it continues to preoccupy them. Furthermore, this thought is complete rubbish. A person can never be a complete failure: If only due to the fact that it would not be possible for a complete failure to be even born. The fact that the person in question is still alive, breathing, can see, can read and write indicates that at least a number of functions are succeeding. A failure is an action or an undertaking which has not succeeded but this cannot be applied to a person as a whole.

Alternative

It is therefore better to pass judgement in terms of specific actions, such as for example: 'I did not manage to lose weight, I did not manage to pass my driving test the first time, but on the other hand I did manage to find a new home within three months' or: 'If I do not achieve some aims that does not mean to say I am a failure

as a person: I have just not managed to do some of the things I wanted to do. I am going to try again or I'll try and do something else.'

8 I hope I'm not going mad

Some worriers get even more panicked by the idea that they will not be able to stop worrying. And then they start to imagine that they will go completely mad (not just 65 per cent but the full 100). 'I hope I'm not going mad' (or 'I hope I'm not going to die, or get a serious illness'). They often add to this: 'I mustn't think about it.' Those who recognize themselves here will doubtless say this is a realistic thought. But it isn't.

The challenge
You won't suddenly go mad just by thinking. Also, what do you understand by mad? Do you mean disturbed, psychotic, out of touch with reality in the psychiatric sense? Do you also picture this being followed by admission to a psychiatric hospital? It is perhaps not impossible that you could drive yourself mad by worrying, but it will take a very long time for this to happen. Most worriers reach pension age without anything like this ever happening. But you could become depressed or anxious or even suicidal by worrying. This is why it is important to deal with your worrying appropriately.

Alternative
'If I carry on worrying a lot, then I will become depressed or anxious, or both. But there is a greater chance that I will just continue to worry as usual and not go mad. I have remained reasonably normal up until now. If I carry on worrying it does not mean that I will then go mad. It is better for me to consider the possibility and take some precautions: I shall try little by little to examine my worries and think of some better alternatives to them.'

Another exercise for readers in the meantime

Below are listed a few more of the most popular worries. For a few of the worries below try to write a challenge and an alternative, in the style of the above examples. Be prepared to sit down and think of reasonable alternatives. By practising these thoughts you can teach yourself to approach your own favourite subjects for worrying.

- I am fat, stupid, ugly and/or unattractive (you choose).
- I have no self-confidence.
- I can't stand up for myself.
- I can never sleep.
- I am of no value to society.

9 Why am I worrying so much?

A favourite occupation of many worriers is to continually ask themselves why they are worrying so much and so often. In the long term this preoccupation can become so overwhelming that they start to worry about the fact that they are worrying. Worriers can end up spending quite a lot of time on this worry. What is striking about those who spend a lot of time on this is that they are often not interested in the most obvious answer: you worry because you are afraid of a future negative event or a negative emotion, and you think incorrectly that by worrying you will have control over the future. The more people worry, the more they are unable to come to any decisions.

The challenge

It is not at all important to know why you are worrying. It is much more important to accept that you are worrying. The drive to find out why you are worrying could keep you busy for several years without you making much progress on this. Have you accepted that you are afraid of the future? Why are you afraid of the future? Because you are afraid that you are going to feel anxious or that

things are going to happen that you don't want to happen. Or perhaps you are afraid that you yourself or the events in your life are not under your control. Maybe you are afraid that you will not be able to express yourself, that you may make a mistake or that you will make some other blunder. If you examine such anxieties more closely, then you will see that these are not at all necessary. For the most part people deal with setbacks much better than they may have previously thought possible. Mostly people can also cope much better than they think with the accompanying emotions. Therefore you do not have to be quite so terrified about your future emotions. Also people are often much better able to do difficult things (such as giving a speech) than they think. By continually worrying about things in advance you will not improve your future performance, but what you will do is waste a lot of time on unnecessary anxiety.

Alternative

'As soon as I say to myself that it is important to know why I worry so much then I will remind myself that it is not at all important to know this or to spend much time dwelling on it. What is more important is how I can stop it. Moreover I do know deep down why I worry: because I am afraid of the future, that is to say I am afraid of what I imagine the future to be. I am therefore afraid of my own thoughts, fantasies and imaginings. My future just exists in my own thoughts. In reality my future could be quite different from what I imagine. This means that it does not make sense to be so afraid of a future which will perhaps be quite different to the one which I now fear.'

10 When will this stop?

A time-consuming preoccupation is 'brooding' over the question as to when the worrying will finally stop. Brooding is continually dwelling on the fact that you are worrying, that you are depressed, or that you are unhappy.

'How long am I going to carry on feeling so bad?' This sort of complaining type of question is rhetorical in character: just one answer is possible and in the imagination of the worrier it is this: 'There will never be an end to this.' Brooding is a form of complaining which is intended to arouse sympathy and at the start this may well actually happen. But after a time this sympathy will wear thin as it will become clear that the person complaining is in fact doing nothing about the cause of the complaint. Because when people complain they are not actually doing anything. Except getting sympathy.

The challenge

If you really want to know how long it will be before the worrying will stop then the answer is quite simple: *It will go on for as long as necessary.* It will go on for as long as it takes to recover from it. A broken leg will take at least six weeks to heal if it is not a complicated break. It takes at least six weeks to recover from excessive worrying, as long as this excessive worrying is not complicated by depression or an anxiety disorder. Otherwise it will take longer. Moreover it is also dependent on the way in which you make this healing process happen. If you do all the exercises in this book seriously and try them out one by one then you will recover more quickly than if you were to think that they were not suitable for you. When you come to realize that excessive worrying is a temporary problem that you can work on by doing the appropriate exercises or having therapy, then recovery will be quicker than if you think that the fact you worry is just one of your character traits.

Alternative

'It will take as long as it takes to recover. If I work on my recovery seriously then it will take me six weeks. Perhaps it may take longer. If I don't do anything about it then it will definitely take longer. Let me try as quickly as possible to change my worrying into a purposeful way of working towards my future.'

11 But that's just the way I am

'I can't change, it's just the way I am.' This is the way worriers who have given up on any attempts to stop worrying think. It is as though they think they have to change their whole personality in order to change their worry habits.

The challenge

This is a good time to discuss this. Some people never worry, others worry a great deal. It is as though worry is a fixed personality trait. Research has shown that what is definite is that people with certain personality traits are more susceptible to excessive worrying. It has been proven that neurotic people are more liable to worry. Neuroticism is an associated character trait which consists of the inclination to react with anxiety, dejection, insecurity, black and white thinking, perfectionism and fear of failure to events in life. It is stressed that this is sometimes a hereditary biological factor. But it is important to note that within the large group of people with a neurotic personality by no means all of them will worry endlessly. Neuroticism cannot be changed but worrying as a form of expression is definitely something that can be changed, either as a result of self-help or therapy. In short, even if you are inclined to be neurotic you can still make changes to your worrying.

Alternative

'I do not have to change in every way if I want to stop worrying. Worrying only relates to a small part of my personality and it's just a bad habit. I can change it if I want to. I have also had periods in my life when I have not worried or when I have worried less, so why should it not be like that again? And when I think that I have always been a worrier, then this means that even I was able to push my worries away. At least for half the time.'

12 I must stop thinking like this

If you have done everything to stop worrying and it hasn't worked, then you can go as far as saying that you have developed a strong desire to stop these thoughts. If you haven't slept for a few days or longer and your thoughts keep going round your head then it is only human to despair and to wonder if you will ever be free of them. Some people succeed in doing this more or less temporarily by drinking a lot of alcohol. Some people try to influence their thoughts by taking cannabis or other consciousness-altering drugs. For the most part, dulling or stopping your thoughts does not work and the remedy is worse than the problem. Once the drugs have come out of your system your thoughts will seem worse than before. A handful of sleeping pills can help you to switch off from your thoughts for a while but it is guaranteed they will return and the following day you will still be crippled by worry. Bear in mind that you can make things worse by saying: 'I *must* stop these thoughts, I can't bear them any longer. If I have to think them for another five minutes then I will go completely mad' or similar things. If you have got to this stage then you have become depressed and possibly also suicidal. By this we mean that you want to rid yourself of these thoughts so much that you are even considering ending your life.

The challenge

If you continuously repeat; 'I want to stop these thoughts' then there will come a point when you can think no thoughts other than these. All other thoughts are pushed out by this one prevailing thought. You are then forced into thinking of ways to stop your thoughts and each of these ways just leads to more problems. You may possibly feel so bad that on impulse you will want to do something drastic to stop these terrible thoughts. You may want to hurt yourself, scratch yourself or harm yourself in another way, take pills, or make attempts to end your life.

All these remedies are worse than the problem. In fact the solution lies elsewhere: *first accept your thoughts for what they are*. You can in reality tolerate your thoughts and you don't have to stop them at this point. Bear in mind: *they are just thoughts*. When you think about wanting to stop these thoughts, what you need to do is to accept that you have these thoughts and that they are a sign that all is not well with you. But you can still live perfectly well with these thoughts. If you just go and sit down and accept you have these thoughts, then you will see that in fact nothing happens at all. Then you can examine your thoughts one by one and try, preferably with someone you trust or a psychologist, to challenge your thoughts one by one and to look for better alternatives (see below). Bear in mind that it is very hard to change all your thoughts in one go. But if you start with some of the main thoughts (such as: 'I have no more future, life will never be happy again') and find better alternatives for them then you will have taken a step in the right direction.

Alternative

'I accept that at the moment I have thoughts which I feel are terrible. I want to stop having them but that won't happen all at once. I am going to try and examine some of my thoughts and look for some better alternatives. If necessary I shall seek help with this from a person I trust, my GP, a telephone helpline or a psychologist. I accept that the thoughts I have mean that not all is well with me. I am perhaps getting depressed by this. If that is the case then my thoughts are coloured by this depression and they are very black and white. This means I can no longer make good judgements about my future. Every time I think: "I *must* stop these thoughts because they have become intolerable", then I will say to myself: "I *want* to stop these thoughts and I am going to work on this, but I can in fact tolerate them."'

Every time you are on the point of doing something like swallowing pills or other things to shut out the thoughts say to yourself: '*Not now, but later*. I am first going to seek help with

examining my thoughts one by one, challenging them and improving on them.'

13 It would be better if I wasn't here any more/I'm a burden to others

At a given moment you could get so desperate with worry that you think it would be much better for yourself and for others if you were no longer there. Perhaps you have thoughts like: 'My friends and family are just fed up with me' or 'I'm just a burden to my children' or 'Why would they want anything to do with me, I'm just moody and depressed and I'm a burden to my loved ones, so it would be better if I was out of the way.'

Thoughts of this type are obviously very common in people who make suicide attempts and people who are depressed. But these are worries which don't add up. What is almost never true is the thought that nobody would care if you were to commit suicide. Some worriers who are depressed will say: 'If I'm not around any more, then nobody will be upset, nobody cares about me and they won't even miss me. They'll get over their grief really quickly.' If you recognize these thoughts or others like them, you need to realize you are suffering from severe depression and that this statement is completely wrong. You have become locked into your own way of thinking which bears no relation to reality. The reality is quite different: those who are close to you in the future could suffer long-term trauma due to your suicide and they may grieve for many years. Even if you believe this is nothing to do with you, it is still true.

The challenge

We know in general that these thoughts don't add up. In the majority of cases, your committing suicide is the last thing they want.

If you were to put it to your friends, family or children, they may well at the most say that you can be rather tiresome with all

your worries and that perhaps you can be rather wearisome with your depressive outlook on life but they would much rather you were still there with them. Given the choice, most family members will say that they would rather be stuck with you still sitting there even though you can be a bit of a pain sometimes. Or they will say that the extent of the burden you may put on them is really actually manageable, and that you should not blame yourself for being depressed and that they would want to support anyone who is sick. What is most important, however, is to be aware that if you were to commit suicide then your loved ones would grieve a great deal and your suicide would be a far greater burden. Moreover, your suicide would cause much more distress to your loved ones than you may now be causing them with your worrying and depression. In short: you would do much better by staying around rather than leaving them.

Alternative

'Other people may definitely find my worrying and my depressive outlook on life tiresome to deal with. But the same could be said if I had a broken leg or if I have had to be cared for by my loved ones because of long-term illness. They are probably happy that they are able to help me out if I am sick. I will try to be as little trouble to my loved ones as possible by working towards a quick recovery and also by changing my worry habits. If I were to commit suicide, then I really will place a great burden on my loved ones, and I don't want to do that. If I do not feel that my loved ones would grieve if I were to die, then I am aware that I am seriously depressed and that this thought is not true. I will try to be less depressive in my outlook.'

14 Life won't get any better/I have no future/Life has no meaning

One group of persistent worriers are inclined to repeat one or more of the following thoughts: 'Is there still any meaning to life?', 'Life

won't get any better' or: 'I have no future any more.' For those who recognize these thoughts, it is important to check how frequently you repeat them to yourself in the space of a day. If you repeat them to yourself more than ten times a day then you are well on the way to suffering from depression or you already are. Depressed people can repeat the same thoughts in an endless litany, sometimes with not much variation on the theme. The question is, what is the effect exactly of such endless repetition? Why would you repeat the same thoughts to yourself ten times or more? Does it make life more meaningful? The core of the problem here is that the more frequently you say this thought to yourself the truer it will seem and the more you will continue to believe in it. But such thoughts are not true.

The challenge

The question about the meaning of life is a typical 'all or nothing' question: Does life have any meaning or not? It is 100 per cent or 0 per cent. Often worriers cannot see any middle ground where life may have meaning 40 per cent of the time and no meaning 60 per cent of the time. But if you ask what people how exactly they are defining the meaning of life you will not get an exact definition. This is in fact impossible anyway as the *meaning of life* is a catch-all expression: it can include everything but there is nothing to accurately describe what the meaning of life covers. People who never think about the meaning of life also have great difficulty in defining it. The question about the meaning of life is rhetorical: the answer can only be negative. In short: asking a question about the meaning of life in itself has no meaning. The question about whether you have any future is from the same stable. It is also a rhetorical question which you are better off not asking.

Of course you will have both good and bad experiences in the future. You will not know now whether parts of your life will be better in the future. You will see that for yourself.

Alternative

'It is better if I do not ask how much meaning my life has. That is because this is a question which has no answer. I will try and get as much satisfaction as possible from the small things I do. I don't know how my future will turn out. There will doubtless be happier and less happy times in my life. I cannot predict the future. I will try as hard as I can to achieve my aims. I do not know to what extent I will succeed in this but I will see this clearly for myself.'

Treatment of obsessive worrying about suicide

Elements from cognitive treatment of worrying may be applied in the treatment of suicidal thoughts. The most important aspect of this is that worry is concentrated into fixed periods during the day.

Fixed times to think about suicide

Mrs. A came for treatment via a series of healthcare professionals, because for years she had been thinking of nothing other than suicide. In reality she did not want to commit suicide at all but her thoughts tortured her to such an extent that she did not see any other way out. She is currently seriously depressed. She has been diagnosed with a borderline personality disorder but at the moment she is more of a depressive. In the past she has made several suicide attempts. Her referral states that she has obsessive compulsive disorder with obsessive worrying about suicide. She continually imagines in her head how she is going to jump off a roof, or jump in front of a train, slash her wrists or take an overdose. These imaginings are repeated continuously without a break. Mrs. A, who is aged 33, is experiencing intense self-loathing. She hates herself. This relates to the different negative experiences she has had throughout her upbringing. She predominantly repeats the following thoughts:

- I don't want to take this any longer.
- I can't enjoy anything any more.
- I just can't bear to think about it.
- When I am no longer here, I won't be a burden to anyone any more.
- I can't stand it any longer.
- I don't see the point of anything any more.
- I can't imagine that anyone can possibly like me.

Admittedly she repeats each of these thoughts more than 500 times a day. She becomes completely exhausted by this. She tries to stop these thoughts but the harder she tries to stop them the more intensely they recur each time. The following instructions have been provided in order to help her to bring these thoughts under control to some extent:

Instructions

Dear Mrs. A. Perhaps you could try the following. Instead of stopping your thoughts, it is perhaps better not to stop them but just to postpone them until specific times. When you try to stop these thoughts, they always come back. They come back in the same way the thought of a pink elephant will when you least want it to. That is to say, if I promise to give you a thousand euros if you don't think about a pink elephant for the next five minutes, then there is a very good chance that you won't be able to manage it. Then you may well notice that the thought about the pink elephant keeps on coming back into your mind. This is the same with everything you may try to stop or to forbid yourself from doing. Therefore I am suggesting to you that you do think about suicide now but in a good way. That is to say: not all day long but at fixed times. What I suggest you do is to set aside a number of hours a day to think about suicide, and nothing else, and then use this time to do so. If you are able to think about suicide for an hour three times a day, and think about it rather less in between these times,

then you will perhaps in total spend several hours less thinking about suicide. Then you will have more free time to spend on other things. The trick is that if you give yourself permission to think about suicide in the next worry time, you will then feel the need to think about suicide less in the time between the worry times. You can then think with peace of mind about the fact that tomorrow morning you can think about suicide again or this evening after dinner. Then you can accommodate your need to think about suicide but you won't have to spend the whole day doing it.

I would suggest that you go and sit down for an hour; at a table with a notepad to hand. Make sure that you won't be disturbed, that your mobile is switched off and that you can devote yourself fully to thinking about suicide. Take a kitchen timer with you and set it for an hour and stop thinking about suicide when this goes off. If you feel that you have still not quite finished then resolve to continue with this train of thought in the next worry time.

If I have understood you correctly, you are spending around eighteen hours a day thinking about suicide, about how you imagine committing suicide and on thoughts such as: I can't stand it any longer, I can't imagine how anyone could possibly like me, etc. If you can now concentrate these thoughts into one hour three times a day, then the result would be that you gain fifteen hours a day to spend doing something else other than think. Because to be honest, I don't think it really matters whether you now spend eighteen hours a day or three hours a day thinking about suicide. Is three hours a day not ample time in which to think about suicide? And in the other fifteen hours of the day am I to assume that you are always coming up with more new and creative thoughts about suicide?

When you practise this exercise, you will then teach yourself that you can start to think about suicide and that you can then stop and postpone your thoughts until another time. Then you are no longer being pushed around by your thoughts but you will have regained some control over them.

The aim is that you think about suicide less in the meantime. This will not be easy to start with but just try it. You can also try to write down the thoughts that come into your head by noting down keywords associated with them on a sheet of paper, which you can then keep until the following worry time. If you do have to go off in the meantime and think intensely about suicide, then this is nothing to be concerned about. Just try to postpone your thoughts to the following worry time.

If when you are ready to sit down and worry about suicide and you find no suicidal thoughts come to mind, which is quite possible, then try to pick up the thread of the thoughts you had during the previous worry time, or the thoughts you had yesterday. In most cases you will be able to pick up the thread again quickly.

If you wake up at night and start thinking about suicide, then here too try to write down the thoughts on a notepad in terms of keywords associated with them. Put this note into a shoe box under your bed. The next morning, during your worry time, take all your notes out of the shoe box and you can then use them to consider the thoughts you had.

If you ask yourself what you should go and do between worry times – well, that is entirely up to you. You could perhaps read a book or do a Sudoku puzzle, phone or visit friends or people you know, or else just do nothing and watch TV. You are free to decide. At the start perhaps you will have to get used to the free time you will have by thinking less about suicide. It is a good idea to arrange things to do with other people in order to fill the time together.

When you find you are getting on well with this exercise, you can shorten the worry times to half an hour or a quarter of an hour. You will then gradually become less weighed down by obsessive thoughts of suicide and these thoughts will occur more of your own free will. The objective is thus not to stop you thinking any suicidal thoughts at all but we just hope that you will find them less of a burden in this way.'

In this way Mrs. A has been given instructions on how to reduce the distress caused by her obsessive thoughts about suicide. Some weeks later it appeared that Mrs. A has succeeded in concentrating her thoughts on suicide into several moments a day. Because she did not like being ordered to go and think about suicide she, on her own initiative, reduced the worry times to three sessions of a quarter of an hour each per day. When she felt inclined to think about suicide in the meantime she said to herself: *Not now but later'*. Her permanent carer noticed that she became more active again, attended her activities and that she was much more cheerful. And she talked noticeably less about suicide.

Of course it is not always like this. In contrast to this success story there are also cases where progress is slower and not as good. But this is one of the possible options which can be tried in cases of chronic and obsessive suicidal thoughts.

Does this sound familiar?

If you the reader recognize elements from the above account, would you like to try out these instructions for yourself?

Worrying in metaphors and with exaggeration

Many worries are in the form of metaphors. For example the thought: 'I am buried alive here in this suburb'. The man who said this of course was not buried but he worded it as though he was. That is a metaphor. He was thus expressing how serious he found the situation, namely very serious. And all metaphors are characterized by slight or more than slight exaggeration. The man was not in fact buried at all but very much alive. But because he let this thought run through his head all day, he ended up feeling down in the dumps (another metaphor). There are many sayings which when repeatedly used can turn into worries. For example: 'They treated me like an idiot' or 'I'll be nothing more than a cabbage in the nursing home.' The metaphor is clear but it is of

course just a manner of speaking. There are no actual cabbages sitting in nursing homes, and only a few people there can no longer communicate much with anyone around them. The word cabbage is used by way of exaggeration.

Real worriers will, without even noticing, start to believe in their exaggerations and accept them as the truth: 'When I have to go into a nursing home I'll end up turning into a cabbage.' That seems a dreadful picture of the future, but it is of course an exaggeration and a fantasy.

Many worriers are characterized by the fact that they no longer use these exaggerated metaphors figuratively but literally, and they end up believing them. For example, the chairman of a technical commission of a volleyball club was not asked to continue by the board once his two-year term was up. He felt he had been treated so unfairly that he referred to it as follows: 'They've *demoted* me.' And he was unable to sleep for weeks due to the unfair treatment he felt he had received. It took a lot of persuasion to convince this man that the word 'demoted' had quite different associations, which were not at all appropriate to his situation. Once he understood how much he had over-exaggerated the situation by referring to it in this way, he could sleep soundly again. What had happened to him was really not that unfair. The moral of this story is that it is not uncommon for worriers to exaggerate greatly and that they then go on to believe in their own exaggerations.

Worrying as self-protection and self-torture

Now we have come to the end of the book, it is logical to once again take some time to look at the function of worrying. Why do people worry so much and so often? What, in the psychological sense, is the explanation for this phenomenon? It is the author's opinion that at best worrying may be understood as an unsuccessful form of self-protection. Worriers try to influence their future, they try to prevent possibly harmful events or situations. In doing this they are actually busy protecting

themselves against future disaster. Worrying can therefore be described as a form of self-protection. People prepare for fight or flight, but the worrier does neither – he just freezes. Somehow in the process of self-protection, worriers get into a state and get caught in a net of repetitive thoughts of the 'all or nothing' type. They end up exaggerating things with metaphors and finally come to a complete standstill. This standstill is then experienced as torture because they feel powerless, without options and without hope. The thoughts just keep coming again and again, and in the end they become a form of self-punishment. This is why excessive worrying is both a form of self-protection and self-torture. Normal worrying can be regarded as self-protection but excessive worrying, on the other hand, is self-protection which has overshot the mark by a long way. This is when it becomes self-torture. We recommend that those who want to be freed from this torture read this book from cover to cover again and above all do the exercises.

Final exercises

For readers who want to do some more exercises to enable them to stop worrying here are a few last tips:

1 *Divide by two*

If you cling onto persistent worries, you will frequently get very negative feelings which go with the frequently exaggerated ideas. If you complain that you are being 'buried alive' then you will end up feeling down in the dumps. If you complain about being *demoted* then you will not feel good about this. If you think that life has no meaning then you will start to feel dejected. In order to bring these feelings back into proportion, you can try to *divide your feelings and thoughts by two*. Just try to divide the feeling of having been treated unfairly by two, so that you still have half of the unpleasant sensation and ask yourself whether half of the intensity of feeling would not be enough in terms of what has happened to you. I would advise our chairman: try to find another

word that has half the impact of 'demoted'. For example: 'The board saw reasons why my contribution would no longer be required.

If you feel that life has no meaning, then try to divide this feeling by two: 'The good part of my life does have meaning, but the other half doesn't (here you could regard the less good half as the half you spend worrying). If you complain about being 'buried alive' divide this by two as well: 'I am not yet buried, I've only got one foot in the grave'.

Another piece of advice would be to divide your worry time in half. If you spend on average six hours a day worrying, then divide this by two and try not to worry for more than three hours a day. Remember that in three hours you cannot worry as much as you can in six, but if you take a thorough approach to it, you will find three hours is more than enough.

2 So what?

The last exercise we will discuss is the 'So what?' exercise. This can be really helpful. What this involves is that for every anxiety that you have about whatever may go wrong in the future, you then ask the question: 'So what?' (or if you want you can replace 'So what?' with 'Oh yes?'). And after asking a succession of 'So what?' questions, then imagine what your situation may be one year after the event you fear. For example: 'I am afraid that I won't pass my preliminary exams.' 'So what?' 'Then I maybe won't complete my studies.' 'So what?' 'Then I will be a disappointment to my parents.' 'Oh yes?' 'That is very upsetting for them.' 'So what?' 'Then I shall have to study something else or get a job.' 'So what?' 'How will you feel about things in a year's time?' 'Perhaps I will regret that I did not study hard enough. But in the meantime I will have found a way forward which perhaps gives me more satisfaction than the studies which did not really engage me.'

Or another example: 'I am afraid that my wife will leave me.' 'So what?' 'I won't be able to cope with that.' 'So what?' 'Then I'll go mad.' 'Oh yes?' 'That is a disaster.' 'So what?' 'Then I will take

to drink.' 'What then?' 'Then I'll drink myself to death.' 'Oh yes?' By the time you end up asking these questions you will yourself come to understand that you are loading exaggeration upon exaggeration. What will your situation probably be in a year's time? Perhaps you can then say: 'Within a year the worst should be over and I may perhaps have the prospect of a new relationship with a nice woman.' But you can never know anything for sure.

The exercise is intended to help you really examine the consequences of your anxiety closely. What could go wrong if everything that you feared became a reality? In the majority of cases the feared future event may have unpleasant consequences but in the long term even in the most undesirable situations you should be able to see possible options for coping with life in the future and you may also encounter new challenges which could in the end make your life better.

Conclusion

Worrying is a form of self-protection which can find its expression in self-torture. The moral here is that you can protect yourself much better by not worrying excessively. If you don't succeed in reducing your worrying and you have used all the exercises in this book seriously, then it is time to seek specialist help. Your GP can refer you to a psychologist, psychotherapist or psychiatrist. All these specialists are able to give you additional help to reduce your worrying. Don't wait too long before seeking professional help, because if you carry on worrying to the same extent, then you will waste a lot of time, you will not solve your problems and that is often an unpleasant situation to be in. It is common for persistent worriers to be able to solve their problems with worry within six weeks with specialist help. But it can take longer. Our advice is not to wait too long before seeking help.

More information about worrying

Would you like some more information about worrying? Here are some sources recommended by the author:

Books

Butler, G. and Hope, T. (2007) *Manage your Mind*, 2nd edn. Oxford: Oxford University Press.

Leahy, R.L. (2003) *Cognitive Therapy Techniques*. New York: Guilford Press.

Leahy, R.L. (2006) *The Worry Cure*. London: Piatkus.

Nolen Hoeksema, S. (2005) *The Worry Princess*. Archipel.

Tips for those providing specialist help

The exercises in this book are excellent for use at the start of psychotherapy treatment for depressive, burn-out or anxiety disorders. Clients who feel as though they are being kicked around like a football by their own thoughts and emotions will be able to benefit very quickly from these exercises. If clients have to wait for a period of time between being referred for help and their consultation or between their consultation and the start of their treatment, they can in the meantime start to work on their recovery with the help of this book. Previous research concerning people who worry has shown that those who reduce their worrying also see a reduction in anxiety or depression. Research has not yet been carried out into whether this applies in equal measure to in-patients and out-patients. In the case of therapy provided within the practice of the author, reductions in depression and anxiety have regularly been noted after active use of these anti-worry exercises.

References

Anderson, L., Lewis, G., Araya, R., Elgie, R., Harrison, G., Proudfoot, J., Schmidt, U., Sharp, D., Weightman, A. and Williams, C. (2005) 'Self-help books for depression: how can practitioners and patients make the right choice?' *British Journal of General Practitioners*, 55: 387–92.

Beck, A.T., Rush, A.J., Shaw, B.F. and Emery, G. (1979) *Cognitive Therapy of Depression*. New York: The Guilford Press.

Boer, P.C. den, Wiersma, D. and Van den Bosch, R.J. (2004) 'Why is self-help neglected in the treatment of emotional disorders? A meta-analysis', *Psychological Medicine*, 34: 959–71.

Borkovec, T. D. (1994) 'The nature, functions, and origins of worry', in G. Davey and F. Tallis (eds) *Worrying: Perspectives on Theory, Assessment and Treatment*. Chichester: Wiley, pp. 5–33.

Borkovec, T.D. and Costello, E. (1993) 'Efficacy of applied relaxation and cognitive behavioral therapy in the treatment of generalized anxiety disorder', *Journal of Consulting and Clinical Psychology*, 61: 611–19.

Borkovec, T.D., Depree, J.A., Pruzinsky, T. and Robinson, E. (1983) 'Preliminary exploration of worry: some characteristics and processes', *Behaviour Research and Therapy*, 21: 9–16.

Borkovec, T.D. and Inz, J. (1990) 'The nature of worry in generalized anxiety disorder: a predominance of thought activity', *Behaviour Research and Therapy*, 28: 153–8.

Borkovec, T.D. and Newman, M.G. (1999) 'Worry and generalized anxiety disorder', in A.S. Bellack, M. Hersen, and Salkovskis (eds) *Comprehensive Clinical Psychology*, vol. 4: *Adults*. Oxford: Elsevier Science, pp. 439–59.

Borkovec, T.D. and Roemer, L. (1995) 'Perceived functions of worry

among generalized anxiety disorder subjects: distraction from more emotionally distressing topics?' *Journal of Behavior Therapy and Experimental Psychiatry*, 26: 25–30.

Borkovec, T.D. and Sharpless, B. (2004) 'Generalized anxiety disorder: Bringing cognitive-behavioral therapy into the valued present', in S.C. Hayes, V.M. Folette, and M.M. Linehan (eds) *Mindfulness and Acceptance: Expanding the Cognitive-behavioral Tradition*. New York: Guilford, pp. 209–42.

Broderick, P.C. (2005) 'Mindfulness and coping with dysphoric mood: contrasts with rumination and distraction', *Cognitive Therapy and Research*, 29: 501–10.

Brosschot, J.F., Gerin, W. and Thayer, J.F. (2006) 'The perseverative cognition hypothesis: a review of worry, prolonged stress-related physiological activation, and health', *Journal of Psychosomatic Research*, 60: 113–24.

Brosschot, J.F. and Van der Doef, M. (2006) 'Daily worrying and somatic health complaints: testing the effectiveness of a simple worry reduction intervention', *Psychology and Health*, 21: 19–31.

Butler, G. (1994) 'Treatment of worry in generalized anxiety disorder', in G. Davey and F. Tallis (eds) *Worrying: Perspectives on Theory, Assessment and Treatment*. Chichester: Wiley, pp. 209–27.

Chelminski, I. and Zimmerman, M. (2003) 'Pathological worry in depressed and anxious patients', *Journal of Anxiety Disorders*, 17: 533–46.

Cuijpers, P. (1997) 'Bibliotherapy in unipolar depression', *Journal of Behavioural Therapy and Experimental Psychiatry*, 28: 139–47.

Davey, G. and Tallis, F. (1994) *Worrying: Perspectives on Theory, Assessment and Treatment*. Chichester: Wiley.

Davey, G.C.L. and Wells, A. (2006) *Worry and its Psychological Disorders: Theory, Assessment, and Treatment*. Chichester: Wiley.

Dugas, M.J., Gagnon, F., Ladouceur, R. and Freeston, M.H. (1998)

'Generalized anxiety disorder: a preliminary test of a conceptual model', *Behaviour Research and Therapy*, 36: 215–26.

Foekema, H. (2001) *Een ieder lijdt het meest . . .* Amsterdam: Nipo.

Fresco, D.M., Frankel, A.N., Mennin, D.S., Turk, C.L. and Heimberg, R.G. (2002) 'Distinct and overlapping features of rumination and worry: the relationship of cognitive production to negative affect states', *Cognitive Therapy and Research*, 26: 179–88.

Hayes, S.C. (2005) *Get Out of Your Mind and into Your Life*. Oakland, CA: New Harbinger Publications.

Hazlett-Stevens, H. (2005) *Women Who Worry Too Much*. Oakland, CA: New Harbinger Publications.

Hermans, H. (2006) *Je piekert je suf*, 9th edn. Amsterdam: Boom.

Hong, R.Y. (2007) 'Worry and rumination: Differential associations with anxious and depressive symptoms and coping behavior', *Behaviour Research and Therapy*, 45: 277–90.

Kerkhof, A.J.F.M., Hermans, D., Figee, A., Laeremans, I., Pieters, G., and Aardema, A. (2000) 'De Penn State Worry Questionnaire en de Worry Domains Questionnaire: eerste resultaten bij Nederlandse en Vlaamse klinische en poliklinische populaties', *Gedragstherapie*, 33(2): 135–45.

Ladouceur, R., Dugas, M.J., Freeston, M.H., Léger, E., Gagnon, F.,and Thibodeau, N. (2000) 'Efficacy of a cognitive-behavioral treatment for generalized anxiety disorder: evaluation in a controlled clinical trial', *Journal of Consulting and Clinical Psychology*, 68(6): 957–64.

Leahy, R.L. (2002) 'Improving homework compliance in the treatment of generalized anxiety disorder', *Journal of Clinical Psychology*, 58: 499–511.

Leahy, R.L. (2003) *Cognitive Therapy Techniques: A Practitioner's Guide*. New York: The Guilford Press.

Leahy, R.L. (2006) *The Worry Cure: Stop Worrying and Start Living*. London: Piatkus Ltd.

Leahy, R.L. and Holland, S.J. (2000) *Treatment Plans and Interventions for Depression and Anxiety Disorders*. New York: Guilford.

Muris, P., Roelofs, J., Rassin, E., Franken, I., and Mayer, B. (2005) 'Mediating effects of rumination and worry on the links between neuroticism, anxiety and depression', *Personality and Individual Differences*, 39: 1105–11.

Nolen-Hoeksema , S. (2003) *Women Who Think Too Much*. New York: Holt and Co.

Segal, Z.V., Williams, M.J.G., and Teasdale, J.D. (2002) *Mindfulness-based Cognitive Therapy for Depression: A New Approach to Preventing Relapse*. New York: Guilford.

Spek, V., Cuijpers, P., Nyklicek, I., Riper, H., Keyzer, J. and Pop, V. (2006) 'Internet based cognitive behaviour therapy for symptoms of depression and anxiety: a meta-analysis', *Psychological Medicine* (doi:10.1017/S0033291706008944).

Sterk, F. and Swaen, S. (2004) *Leven met een piekerstoornis* (How to Live with a Worry Disorder). Houten: Bohn Stafleu Van Loghum.

Stöber, J. and Bittencourt, J. (1998) 'Weekly assessment of worry: adaptation of the Penn State Worry Questionnaire for monitoring changes during treatment', *Behaviour Research and Therapy*, 36: 645–56.

Tallis, F. (1990) *How to Stop Worrying*. London: Sheldon Press.

Tallis, F. and Eysenck, M.W. (1994) 'Worry: mechanisms and modulating influences', *Behavioural and Cognitive Psychotherapy*, 22: 37–56.

Watkins, E., Moulds, M., and Mackintosh, B. (2005) 'Comparisons between rumination and worry in a non-clinical population', *Behaviour Research and Therapy*, 43: 1577–85.

Wells, A. (2000) *Emotional Disorders and Metacognition*. Chichester: Wiley.

Wells, A. and Papageorgiou, C. (1995) 'Worry and the incubation of intrusive images following stress', *Behaviour Research and Therapy*, 33: 579–83.

Praise for this book

'CBT requires a measure of self-discipline that can be hard to muster when you're struggling. The real strength of this book is that it's structured day by day programme that tells you exactly what to do when.'

'This is not just a collection of good ideas but a carefully structured programme that should yield real benefits for anyone who follows it. Professor Kerkhof offers practical exercises using techniques clinically proven to help in the management of anxiety.'

'This is a wise, practical book full of genuinely useful strategies for dealing with your worries.'
Dr Stephen Briers, Clinical psychologist and broadcaster

It's good to see a self-help book which is based on solid, psychological research. It's a book which sets realistic goals, has a down-to-earth approach and is genuinely useful. This book is careful not to promise the earth, but if the exercises are followed carefully some people will find it makes a real difference.
Claudia Hammond, Broadcaster and writer

Very simple and very practical.
Professor Geoff Beattie, University of Manchester and resident Big Brother psychologist

Contents

Foreword

Excessive worrying is a burdensome phenomenon which can considerably affect the lives of the people who struggle with it. People with depression or depressive disorders, for example, have to deal with this to a far greater extent than others. In some cases people who worry excessively even go on to develop what may be referred to as a 'worry disorder' which can seriously disrupt their lives. In the United Kingdom around 4.4 per cent of adults suffer from a worry disorder (also referred to as a 'generalized anxiety disorder'). Exactly how many people suffer from excessive worrying is not known precisely but it must be around several hundred thousand a year. There is thus no doubt that this is a very frequently occurring phenomenon.

It is therefore commendable that a book has now appeared for people who suffer from excessive worrying. One of the most positive aspects of this book is that it offers a wide range of exercises that people can do themselves to reduce worrying. People who struggle with worrying can quite satisfactorily tackle worry for themselves. We also know this from a number of scientific studies. This book offers a rich and varied choice of exercises which worriers can do for themselves. If one tackles this seriously, there is a good chance that the worrying will be considerably reduced.

This book has been written by Professor Ad Kerkhof and his colleagues. He is not only a highly valued colleague of mine but also an experienced clinician. Professor Kerkhof has many years experience as a psychotherapist and has used this experience to produce this book. And as you will see, the exercises are easy to do but still structured in an effective and balanced way.

As well as being a clinician, Prof. Kerkhof is also an excellent

researcher/academic who well knows what research into the
treatment of worrying has produced, as you will see in this book.
This book is based on the principles of cognitive behavioural
therapy which we know is very effective when dealing with
worrying. Moreover, the information is presented in such a way
that people can adapt the exercises to their own needs.

All in all, this is an excellent book which I would very much like
to recommend to people who want to get to grips with and change
their excessive worrying.

Professor Pim Cuijpers
Amsterdam
Autumn 2007

Guidance note

This self-help book contains a number of exercises to do at home. These are exercises which you can also do anywhere, in the car or while doing the shopping. These exercises will slowly but surely help you to worry less. What you will have to do is to set aside a quarter of an hour twice a day in which you commit to do the exercises. This is a time investment which you will quickly recoup as you will spend less time worrying. You should also aim to do the exercises at weekends.

In this book of exercises there are one or more exercises for each day. We advise you to go through this book of exercises step by step and to calmly take the time to try out each exercise. After a while, you will notice which exercises work best for you. And then you can select a number of different exercises. If you find you are at times still worrying after completing this course, then you can of course always continue using the exercises in this book.

Worrying often happens automatically without us necessarily being aware of it. If you concentrate on this activity, you may notice your worrying thoughts may occur more frequently than you were previously aware of. Then it may also seem that at the start you are worrying more. After some time, however, you should notice that you are overtaken by worrying thoughts less frequently.

This exercise book will not solve your problems. You will, however, learn to worry less about your problems. This will free up time for you to work on real solutions.

We wish you every success and perhaps even some fun with the exercises!

Professor Ad Kerkhof   Saida Akhnikh   Anneke Koopman
Maarten van der Linde   Marleen Stam   Elvan Tutkun

The Cognitive Behavioural Therapy approach to worrying

For those clients (and therapists) who want to know how this book works, some scientific background material is provided in the next couple of pages. Readers who don't want to read this now can proceed immediately to the beginning of the book on page 1.

The Cognitive Behavioural Therapy (CBT) model emphasizes that emotional states, depression, anger and suicidal thoughts are often maintained and strengthened by exaggerated or biased ways of thinking. In therapy, clients are taught how to improve their thinking habits. In CBT, thinking habits which are frequently encountered, such as generalization, selective attention, catastrophizing, are being combated with a multitude of CBT techniques. Nowadays it is increasingly clear that in order to benefit from CBT approaches clients do not even have to see a therapist face to face. E-mental health approaches (web-based self-help interventions), bibliotherapy, or e-mail chat therapy can work as well.

Worrying is a stream of often uncontrollable stressful recurrent negative thoughts, mostly anticipating and expecting negative outcomes in the future, focused on control and avoidance of future danger or failure. Worry is a central element in generalized anxiety, post-traumatic stress and depression (Borkovec et al. 1983; Borkovec 1994; Borkovec and Sharpless 2004; Chelminski and Zimmerman 2003; Kerkhof et al. 2000). Worrying and rumination, closely related but distinct processes (Fresco et al. 2002; Watkins et al., 2005; Hong 2007), are associated with general health complaints, cardiovascular disease and also with cardiovascular, endocrinological and immunological activation (Brosschot and Van

der Doef 2006; Brosschot et al. 2006). There is an abundance of research linking worrying to neuroticism (Davey and Tallis 1994; Tallis and Eysenck 1994; Muris et al. 2005). Excessive worrying may be one of the accelerators of anxiety and depression, but it may also be conceived of as a product of anxiety and depression.

Even milder forms of excessive worrying are troublesome and can induce sleeplessness and stress. From a preventive, public health approach, there are several popular books to help people reduce their unwanted worrying, which will thus also prevent the development of more serious clinical syndromes (e.g. Nolen-Hoeksema 2003; Tallis 1990; Sterk and Swaen 2004; Leahy 2006; Hayes 2005). Readers may find tips and advice on how to deal with recurrent intrusive thoughts such as rumination or worrying. As yet there are not many experimental studies focusing exclusively on the psychological treatment of non-clinical worrying. Most of the research into the treatment of worrying has concentrated on patients with General Anxiety Disorder (Ladouceur et al. 2000).

Self-help interventions are effective in reducing mental health problems in the general population (Anderson et al. 2005; Boer et al. 2004; Cuijpers, 1997). A self-help intervention is a structured psychological treatment which the person works through independently at home. Self-help interventions may be accessible in writing (bibliotherapy), on CD-ROM, on video or DVD, through television programmes, or over the internet (Spek et al. 2006). Self-help interventions may reach people in the general population who are not seeking, or do not yet seek or find professional mental health care.

In a Dutch adult community study, 9 per cent of respondents reported excessive worry. This means that about 1.1 million Dutch adults are suffering to some degree. Those with excessive worrying reported negative effects on their mental health, more days on sick leave (30 days versus 12 days a year), more GP visits (7 vs 3), higher use of tranquillizers (35 per cent vs 9 per cent) and antidepressants (22 per cent vs 3 per cent) (Foekema 2001). From

this study it is clear that although excessive worriers do receive more medical care and mental health care, many do not receive adequate help or treatment and they can find themselves worrying for extended periods of time. Therefore we felt a need to develop a structured self-help approach to provide people in the community with tools to combat initial stages of excessive worrying and in doing so to prevent people having to access mental health care. It was considered worthwhile to develop a short worry reduction course in writing that would be easy to distribute, through GPs, pharmacies, bookshops, and the internet.

As a general framework for the intervention in this book, we used the model of worrying of Borkovec (Borkovec and Costello 1993; Borkovec and Newman 1999; Borkovec and Roemer 1995), and Dugas, Gagnon, Ladouceur and Freeston (1998), focusing on intolerance of uncertainty, erroneous beliefs about worry, poor problem orientation and cognitive avoidance. We use these CBT approaches to worrying in combination with problem solving approaches and some mindfulness approaches (Beck et al. 1979; Borkovec et al. 1983, Butler 1994; Leahy and Holland 2000, Leahy 2002, 2003, 2006; Broderick 2005, Segal et al. 2002; Hayes 2005; Hazlett-Stevens 2005; Ladouceur et al. 2000; Wells and Papageorgiou 1995; Wells 2000; Davey and Wells 2006). CBT and problem solving approaches have proved their efficacy in the face-to-face treatment of depression and anxiety, and for other mental health problems. This also applies to CBT self-help approaches. In these interventions the application of CBT to worrying has received considerable attention (Ladouceur et al. 2000; Leahy 2002, 2003, 2006; Wells 2000; Davey and Wells 2006). In the mindfulness-based CBT approaches, worrying is one of the targets for decentring and meditation (Segal et al. 2002).

The general idea of the interventions in this book is that subjects:

- learn to regain control over their thoughts;
- learn to realistically evaluate future threats;

- learn to identify and combat automatic thoughts;
- learn to identify and combat common errors in thinking;
- correct erroneous beliefs about worrying;
- learn to use other means of coping with future threats;
- learn how to deal with uncertainty;
- learn how to face cognitions instead of avoiding cognitions;
- learn how to use distraction, relaxation, writing, imagination, and humour as coping mechanisms.

Exercises chosen or developed for this worry reduction intervention are, among others:

- worry postponement;
- muscle relaxation exercises;
- writing exercises;
- monitoring specific worries;
- using positive forms of worrying;
- meditation/mindfulness-type exercises;
- the use of a buddy to communicate about worries.

Acknowledgements

This self-help book has been produced as the result of a research project where 200 'worriers' read an earlier version. The scientific evaluation and the reactions of the 'worriers' have led to adaptations of and improvements to this book. The question list used to measure the weekly level of worry is the Penn State Worry Questionnaire – Past Week (Stöber and Bittencourt 1998). The daily measurement of worrying and sleeping problems is developed by Chantal Schutz (2002) in her Master's thesis on worrying.

Most of the exercises in this self-help book are new and have been especially created for this project. A small number of the exercises are commonly used cognitive behavioural therapy exercises, such as the relaxation exercises, or mindfulness exercises, such as the whirling with your thoughts exercise.

The exercise with the 7b's on pages 130–31 is an adapted version of the 5b exercise of F. Sterk and S. Swaen, *Living with Worry* (2004: 83).

The exercise with the three columns on pages 110–15 has been reprinted with the permission of H. Hermans, *Je piekert je suf* (2006: 65–6).

I would like to express my gratitude to Anna George for her faithful translation from the original Dutch text, and my special thanks to Dr Monika Lee at Open University Press for all her enthusiasm and support.

About the authors

Ad Kerkhof is Professor of Clinical Psychology at the VU University Amsterdam. He specializes in worry, depression and suicide. Ad Kerkhof also has a psychotherapy practice, where he treats clients for persistent forms of worrying, depression, burn-out and suicidal thoughts. He observed that suicides and suicide attempts are often preceded by persistent worrying and lack of sleep. Since then he has considered suicidal thoughts as an expression of excessive and persistent worrying. This offers new starting points for suicide prevention and the psychotherapy treatment of depressed and suicidal patients. *Stop Worrying* has also been written in the hope that people who worry and read this book will not reach the stage of contemplating suicide.

Saida Akhnikh, Anneke Koopman, Maarten van der Linde, Marleen Stam, and Elvan Tutkun were doctoral students in clinical psychology at the VU University of Amsterdam. They carried out research on the *Stop Worrying* project which formed the basis of this publication.

Part 1

....

Stop worrying in four weeks

What is worry?

Worry is a phenomenon which all of us will have experienced at least once. Who has not on occasion had a sleepless night when they have stayed awake tossing and turning with worry? You will primarily worry about difficult things. For example, about taking a driving test, a dentist's appointment, problems at work, problems in a relationship or a critical remark by a friend. You might worry about the future and also about events in the past. You might even worry about the fact that you are worrying.

Of course, it is necessary to consider how to solve or prevent problems. This only becomes a burden when you can no longer control your thoughts – when they suddenly come into your head at inconvenient moments, when the same thoughts keep on recurring and when you cannot stop them. The majority of worrying thoughts don't lead to a solution. You finish up going round in never-ending circles. You then end up drifting into excessive worrying due to these thoughts.

In the majority of cases, excessive worrying is completely unproductive. It costs time and energy. Excessive worrying about the future often goes hand in hand with anxiety. You have a concern and you always ask: 'What if . . . ?' Your muscles tense unnecessarily and in the long term you feel more and more tired and apathetic. Worrying about things which have happened in the past gives rise to feelings of dejection and anger. Worriers often know perfectly well that they cannot change the past but they still remain caught up in negative memories and can no longer concentrate on school, work or household duties.

Long-term worry can mean that you find it difficult to sleep. Or you are so tired that you go out like a light but after a few hours you are wide awake again . . . and worrying. It is night-time worrying which is often the most troublesome because everything seems worse at night and because the following day you feel even more tired. This can even become so serious that you have no desire to do anything any more. That is a pity and it moreover

gives you occasion to worry all the more. Once you are caught in this vicious circle, it is hard to find a way out.

We thus return to the original question: 'What actually is worry?' Worry is definitely not the same as thinking, it is the uninterrupted never-ending repetition of the same thoughts. Thinking leads to solutions or recovery. Worrying leads nowhere. Thinking leads to action, worrying leads to nothing, at the very most it may lead to preparation for action but then one just freezes, as it were, during these preparations. Thinking leads to relief, worrying does not. Worrying leads to powerlessness. Thinking leads to the energy to take action. Worrying leads to tiredness and exhaustion.

Worry is something which many people experience regardless of their personality. But there are naturally people who never worry and people who often worry. In German, the following words are used for worrying: *Besorgnis* or *grübeln*. From the sound of these words alone it is clear that they don't mean anything good. But the best foreign term for worrying is in French: *torturer l'esprit*, torturing of the mind. Our proposal is that we subscribe to the French viewpoint and that we regard worrying as a form of self-torture.

What can be done about it?

You can use your own strength to ensure you overcome these thoughts. This book of exercises should help you to worry less so that you have more time and energy left to deal with your problems in a different, more focused manner.

What is at the heart of this approach is that you learn as quickly as possible to recognize your worrying thoughts and to replace them with something else. This may be other thoughts but it could also be distraction, relaxation, a thought break or just letting thoughts whirl around freely in your head. You could also learn how to worry in a positive manner. This book offers a number of exercises which have been proven to help you to do this – at

least if you practise them regularly. The most vital requirement is the time to do the exercises and patience, as it will take some time to break the habit of worrying. You are training your thoughts, as it were. Just as with fitness training, repetition and perseverance are required to get results. The most effective strategy is to do one or more tasks every day and thus work through all the exercises. After that you can continue to use the exercises which work best for you.

It sometimes helps to write down worrying thoughts, examine them and consider whether it is perhaps possible to think any other less anxious or gloomy thoughts. You could, for example, write your thoughts in a notebook.

Because many of your worrying thoughts play out in your imagination (for example, what you think the future has in store for you), it is necessary to combat these thoughts with more realistic imaginings. For many exercises you need to fantasize a little, for example, not just about what could go wrong but also what could go right. You should use the power of your imagination in a more realistic direction.

You will also need an old shoebox or rucksack, a good friend, a notepad or notebook, a pen and a kitchen timer. Make sure you are sleeping on a good mattress as a poor quality mattress can lead to a lack of sleep and thus to worry.

At the beginning

When you decide to start doing the exercises in this book, it is good to always bear the following points in mind:

1   Even if you are a worrier by nature, you can still benefit from a considerable reduction in the time you spend worrying.
2   If you imagine that as from tomorrow you will never worry ever again, then you will not succeed. This is unrealistic.
3   If you imagine that once you have reached the end of this book of exercises you will not worry any more, then this can be a

further source of disappointment if you then don't get to that stage. This is probably hoping for too much.

4   If through using this book you aim to halve the time spent worrying, then this is a realistic objective. Who knows, you may reduce it by more than half which would then be a bonus.

5   If you start to consider your worries during the quarter of an hour set aside for this, known as worry time, and nothing comes to mind and you don't succeed in having any worrying thoughts, then you can go back further and deal with what you were worrying about yesterday.

6   If that doesn't work either, there is no need to be concerned. You can do different exercises, for example, relaxation exercises which will help you achieve the desired results.

7   The aim is for you to concentrate your worrying within fixed periods of time, during the worry times.

8   If you notice that during the second week working with the book you are worrying more than in the first week, then this too does not matter at all. Worrying is not something which remains stable every day of the week. It fluctuates in frequency and intensity. The best approach is to accept these changes as normal.

9   The objective is that you regularly record in the exercise book how much and how intensely you worry. This recording of your patterns of worry is one of the most powerful and effective exercises in the book. The better records you keep of how frequently you worry, the better the view you will have of the (lost) time which you spend on this activity and the better you will be able to monitor your progress. Here measurement = knowledge.

10   If you record your progress regularly in this exercise book, then that will help you to do your exercises regularly.

11   If now and again you have an uncontrollable urge to worry, for example because you feel you need to due to a new situation, then it is perhaps best to give in on that one occasion. But don't do this too often.

12 If you notice that you regress on one or a few occasions and you are once again worrying more than during the past few days, this too is nothing to be concerned about. It is completely natural that now and again you will regress to a greater or lesser extent. It is precisely at these times that you need to follow through with the exercises and you should notice over the whole four-week period that you will on average have made progress.

13 If you dislike some of the worry exercises, find them unpleasant or ineffective, then you can upon your own initiative replace these with other exercises – exercises which you find work better for you, earlier exercises from this book or exercises which you think up for yourself, which you have read about elsewhere or which others have told you about.

14 The method described here works and has been proven by scientific research. But it does not work in equal measure for everyone. Some people derive a great deal of benefit from it, others less. And there will be a few who will derive no benefit at all. It cannot be predicted in advance into which category you will fall. You will notice this for yourself.

15 If during the period of the exercises you go on holiday, have to take an exam, have a death or illness in the family and due to these circumstances you cannot practise the exercises for one or more weeks, this does not have to disrupt your efforts to worry less. After several weeks you can pick up from where you left off, or you can start again from scratch, if you feel this is necessary.

16 Worrying is a serious activity. In order to reduce its effects it is important to relativize your worry. You will gradually learn how to do this through the exercises, with a degree of humour, when you look at your own thought patterns. That means that from time to time you will need to treat the exercises detailed here with humour. Anti-worrying exercises don't have to be terribly serious all the time.

17 Don't forget to tell those close to you about your efforts to worry less. They will be happy to support you.

Week
1

To begin with: how much have you worried over the past week?

For each of the following statements indicate which is most applicable to you by circling the appropriate number. This applies to the past week.

		never	very rarely	rarely	some-times	often	very often	almost always
1	If I did not have enough time to do everything, I did not worry about it.	6	5	4	3	2	1	0
2	My worries overwhelmed me.	0	1	2	3	4	5	6
3	I didn't tend to worry about things.	6	5	4	3	2	1	0
4	Many situations made me worry.	0	1	2	3	4	5	6
5	I knew that I shouldn't have worried about things but I just couldn't help it.	0	1	2	3	4	5	6
6	When I was under pressure, I worried a lot.	0	1	2	3	4	5	6
7	I was always worrying about something.	0	1	2	3	4	5	6
8	I found it easy to dismiss worrisome thoughts.	6	5	4	3	2	1	0

Week

1

		never	very rarely	rarely	some-times	often	very often	almost always
9	As soon as I finished one task, I started to worry about everything else that I had to do.	0	1	2	3	4	5	6
10	I did not worry about anything.	6	5	4	3	2	1	0
11	When there was nothing more I could do about a concern, I did not worry about it any more.	6	5	4	3	2	1	0
12	I noticed that I had been worrying about things.	0	1	2	3	4	5	6
13	Once I started worrying, I couldn't stop.	0	1	2	3	4	5	6
14	I worried all the time.	0	1	2	3	4	5	6
15	I worried about projects until they were all done.	0	1	2	3	4	5	6
	Total							

⟫ *Total score for the past week:*

Day 1 *The beginning*

As from today you will not spend all day worrying. Instead you will allocate two fixed worry times, one worry time in the morning or the afternoon and one in the evening. You will use these times to do your exercises. Try to do the exercises at the same time each day.

Worry time I
Controlled worrying
morning/afternoon

Explanation It is important to make worrying as unattractive as possible. So you will no longer go and worry in your warm bed or in your favourite comfortable armchair but you will sit on an upright chair at a table. Instead of being overcome by the worrying thoughts, you will now consciously seek them out and control them in the worry time. If you don't succeed in worrying intensely during the worry time, then this doesn't matter. Go through the other exercises and then try to worry as much as possible during the following worry time.

a First fill in here which fixed time slots you have selected.

Time slot 1 ....

Time slot 2 ....

b For these worry times choose a place where you will not be disturbed. If necessary, lock the door.

c During this worry time, you will worry as much as possible about everything you are concerned about. Once the worry time is up, stop worrying and go and do something else. If you have not yet finished worrying then you can give yourself the

task of continuing with this during the worry time in the evening.

In the meantime   Sometimes you will worry in the meantime. That is not serious but do try as much as possible to keep these worrying thoughts for the next worry time. Here is an exercise which you could do in the meantime if you start to worry: clap your hands loudly and say to yourself, 'Not now!' (and postpone the worrying until the evening).

Worry time II
Positive worrying 1
evening

Explanation   Whenever we worry, we are overtaken by negative thoughts and feelings. This does not serve any purpose. If you are worrying, is there any reason why you should not think about a happy time too? We now replace the negative thoughts and feelings with a positive memory.

a   Just as during the previous worry time, start to worry intensely. But do this for just five minutes.

b   Devote the following ten minutes to a good memory. Ensure you are in a relaxed position. Close your eyes and take a few deep breaths. Go back in your thoughts to an event which made you happy at the time. Think about this as intensely as possible. Look around in your thoughts and pay attention to the small things too. What colours did you see? What kind of noises were there to be heard? Who was there? What did they say? What could you smell at that moment? Go back to this event in your thoughts for ten minutes. We refer to this exercise as positive worrying 1 and we shall use this more frequently: always just think back to a good memory.

Day 1 Notes

1   Tick the boxes to indicate which subjects you have worried about today (you can give several answers).

studies/ work	finances	health	relationships	family/ friends	what others think of me	other
❑	❑	❑	❑	❑	❑	❑

2   Tick a box to indicate how many minutes/hours you have worried today.

0–30 minutes	30–60 minutes	1–2 hours	2–3 hours	3–4 hours	4–5 hours	› 5 hours
❑	❑	❑	❑	❑	❑	❑

3   Tick a box to indicate how much effort it took today to stop worrying, on a scale of 1 (almost no effort) to 5 (a great deal of effort).

no effort at all	almost no effort	some effort	quite a lot of effort	a great deal of effort
❑	❑	❑	❑	❑

4 How did you sleep last night? Indicate to what extent the following three statements apply to you.

	completely true	true	neutral	untrue	not true at all
I found it hard to get to sleep.	1	2	3	4	5
I suffered disturbed or broken sleep.	1	2	3	4	5
I awoke too early.	1	2	3	4	5

5 **Event** Did anything particular happen today which made you start to worry? If so then write down what happened below, using key words.

....

....

....

....

....

....

....

....

....

28
27
26
25
24
23
22
21
20
19
18
17
16
15
14
13
12
11
10
9
8
7
6
5
4
3
2
1

Day 2 *Distraction*

Worry time I
Look for distraction
morning/afternoon

Explanation   You can get out of the vicious circle of worrying thoughts just by doing something to distract yourself. Worrying often makes us somewhat passive. The best remedy is to look for contact with others or to stay active and busy.

Week

1

a   Begin today with ten minutes worrying. Worry as intensely as possible.

b   If you find yourself worrying, you may feel that you cannot stop. One way to stop is to look for some distraction. Today think about what you could do to distract yourself from these thoughts. The best remedy is to look for contact with others.

⟹   Look for contact with others. Have a chat with a neighbour or telephone a friend.
⟹   Get active, or do some sports practise. For example, go for a bike ride or a walk, preferably with someone else.
⟹   Take a nice shower, let all the worry be washed away.
⟹   Read a good book, you will then be in another world.

c   Make a list of distraction activities in your notebook.

In the meantime   When you start to worry, look for some distraction by engaging in the activities you have just listed (for example, calling on someone, telephoning a friend, practising a sport).

Worry time II
Positive worrying 2
evening

Explanation We often concentrate on looking at our negative side and qualities. This gives us a feeling of unease and ensures that all too soon we end up . . . yes you guessed it, worrying! It is important that we emphasize our positive qualities and skills. You will have more than enough of these.

a Start by worrying intensely for five minutes.

b Then do the second positive worrying exercise. Close your eyes. Take a quality or skill which you are good at or in which you take a pride. This could be anything. You stood up for yourself or someone else once, you are a good spouse, parent, colleague or friend, you are a good cook, you can write or dance well, you are amusing, smart. You then say to yourself: 'I am good at . . .' Perhaps you will doubt that you can hold onto this good feeling. So say it again: 'I am good at . . .' Now say it to yourself twenty times. Allow yourself to be proud for five minutes.
     This is what we call positive worrying 2.

At night Are you unable to sleep at night due to all that worrying? If so, there are a number of things that could help you. Before going to sleep you could drink a glass of warm milk, read, listen to music. You could also put on something warm, for example, pyjamas or an extra T-shirt. Try out positive worrying. Think about a happy event or a good quality or skill you have.

Day 2 Notes

1 Tick the boxes to indicate which subjects you have worried about today (you can give several answers).

studies/ work	finances	health	relationships	family/ friends	what others think of me	other
❑	❑	❑	❑	❑	❑	❑

Week

1

2 Tick a box to indicate how many minutes/hours you have worried today.

0–30 minutes	30–60 minutes	1–2 hours	2–3 hours	3–4 hours	4–5 hours	› 5 hours
❑	❑	❑	❑	❑	❑	❑

3 Tick a box to indicate how much effort it took today to stop worrying, on a scale of 1 (almost no effort) to 5 (a great deal of effort).

no effort at all	almost no effort	some effort	quite a lot of effort	a great deal of effort
❑	❑	❑	❑	❑

4 How did you sleep last night? Indicate to what extent the following three statements apply to you.

	completely true	true	neutral	untrue	not true at all
I found it hard to get to sleep.	1	2	3	4	5
I suffered disturbed or broken sleep.	1	2	3	4	5
I awoke too early.	1	2	3	4	5

5 **Event** Did anything particular happen today which made you start to worry? If so then write down what happened below, using key words.

....

....

....

....

....

....

....

....

....

....

28
27
26
25
24
23
22
21
20
19
18
17
16
15
14
13
12
11
10
9
8
7
6
5
4
3
2
1

Day 3 *Concentration*

Worry time I
Concentrating on breathing
morning/afternoon

Explanation   The aim of this exercise is to learn to breathe with the highest level of concentration.

Week

1

You are going to relax in this worry time. Go and sit at the (kitchen) table and relax. Set the kitchen timer for ten minutes. Become conscious of all your movements. Are you moving your foot? Are you sitting so your body is twisted or are you relaxed? Is your jaw relaxed? Are your shoulders relaxed? This exercise sounds very simple but it requires a great deal of concentration. Now you are going to count your breaths. While you are counting your breaths, pay attention to how deeply you are breathing. Pay attention to the point at which breathing in changes into breathing out. This exercise is about breathing purposefully. You will feel that every time you breathe in you become a little larger and every time you breathe out you become a little smaller. Do thoughts come into your mind or do you have intense feelings and are distracted by this? Don't judge yourself because these thoughts occur. Just let this go. Continue to concentrate on your breathing. Do this ten times and repeat.

In the meantime   Try to postpone worrying thoughts until the second worry time. If this does not work, then look for a distraction or do positive worrying exercise 1 about a happy memory or positive worrying exercise 2 about one of your positive qualities.

Worry time II
Slow concentration
evening

Explanation   In this exercise you will carry out an activity on which you will concentrate fully. You will experience how relaxing this can be.

This worry time will be spent carrying out an activity with the highest level of concentration. The activity is, for example, going for a walk. Are you good on your feet and is the weather outside good enough? Then go outside and walk for a quarter of an hour. If you normally go running somewhere, then run at a certain rate. You will run more slowly than normal during this exercise. Run at half your normal speed. Go for a nice stroll. Pay attention to the movement of your body. Are your shoulders relaxed? Make sure your jaw is relaxed while running. Notice how your feet touch the ground. If your attention drifts away from your body, then look at the environment. What can you see around you? Do you see trees, clouds or animals? What buildings can you see, which people? What sounds can you hear around you? Note the thoughts which come to you, 'look' at them and then let them go. You can also carry out this exercise with other activities such as tidying up, washing up, going cycling, etc. The most important element is that you carry out the activity accurately and at half your normal speed.

At night   Perhaps due to tension you lie there tossing and turning with worry. Try to postpone the worrying thoughts until the following worry time. Use the distraction, positive worrying exercise 1 and positive worrying exercise 2.

28
27
26
25
24
23
22
21
20
19
18
17
16
15
14
13
12
11
10
9
8
7
6
5
4
3
2
1

Day 3 Notes

Week

1

1   Tick the boxes to indicate which subjects you have worried about today (you can give several answers).

studies/ work	finances	health	relationships	family/ friends	what others think of me	other
❏	❏	❏	❏	❏	❏	❏

2   Tick a box to indicate how many minutes/hours you have worried today.

0–30 minutes	30–60 minutes	1–2 hours	2–3 hours	3–4 hours	4–5 hours	› 5 hours
❏	❏	❏	❏	❏	❏	❏

3   Tick a box to indicate how much effort it took today to stop worrying, on a scale of 1 (almost no effort) to 5 (a great deal of effort).

no effort at all	almost no effort	some effort	quite a lot of effort	a great deal of effort
❏	❏	❏	❏	❏

4 How did you sleep last night? Indicate to what extent the following three statements apply to you.

	completely true	true	neutral	untrue	not true at all
I found it hard to get to sleep.	1	2	3	4	5
I suffered disturbed or broken sleep.	1	2	3	4	5
I awoke too early.	1	2	3	4	5

5 **Event** Did anything particular happen today which made you start to worry? If so then write down what happened below, using key words.

....

....

....

....

....

....

....

....

....

28
27
26
25
24
23
22
21
20
19
18
17
16
15
14
13
12
11
10
9
8
7
6
5
4
3
2
1

Day 4 *Whirling thoughts*

Worry time I
Whirling exercise
morning/afternoon

Explanation   In this exercise you will learn how to distance yourself from your thoughts. You will learn how to relativize them and how to view them comparatively.

a   Begin with around ten minutes intense worrying.

Week

1

b   Now we will start with a whirling exercise. Try to empty your mind for the whirling exercise. If thoughts come into your mind, don't try to prevent this. Thoughts are just thoughts. Accept everything that comes to mind. Place these thoughts in light clouds. Let these clouds quietly whirl around in your head while you concentrate on your breathing. Let the clouds with thoughts in them move here and there slowly in your head, from left to right and back again. When you breathe out, you can quietly blow the clouds away. In this way you can allow the thoughts to come and then go again. We call this whirling.

In the meantime   If you have worrying thoughts, then postpone these until the next worry time, clap your hands and say to yourself, 'Not now', or do a positive worrying exercise.

Worry time II
Continuation of whirling exercise
evening

a Begin with five minutes worrying.

b We shall take the whirling exercise from the first worry time further. Empty your mind. Try to place the thoughts that come to you in clouds. Think about the fact that these thoughts are not the truth. There are no bad thoughts. You don't have to think the thoughts. You can also allow them to be what they are. You don't have to concentrate on these thoughts, you can let them whirl away. You don't have to finish your thoughts. You don't need to have control over your thoughts. We call this thought whirling too. Carry out this exercise for five minutes.

At night Put a shoebox or an old rucksack under your bed. Every time you wake up and get a worrying thought, put this in your imagination in the box or the rucksack. Close the box or the rucksack and put it back under the bed. Or write the worrying thought down in a tiny memo and place this in your shoebox. The following morning you can get out your worrying thoughts again during the worry time.

28
27
26
25
24
23
22
21
20
19
18
17
16
15
14
13
12
11
10
9
8
7
6
5
4
3
2
1

Day 4 Notes

1   Tick the boxes to indicate which subjects you have worried
    about today (you can give several answers).

studies/ work	finances	health	relationships	family/ friends	what others think of me	other
❏	❏	❏	❏	❏	❏	❏

2   Tick a box to indicate how many minutes/hours you have
    worried today.

0–30 minutes	30–60 minutes	1–2 hours	2–3 hours	3–4 hours	4–5 hours	› 5 hours
❏	❏	❏	❏	❏	❏	❏

3   Tick a box to indicate how much effort it took today to stop
    worrying, on a scale of 1 (almost no effort) to 5 (a great deal
    of effort).

no effort at all	almost no effort	some effort	quite a lot of effort	a great deal of effort
❏	❏	❏	❏	❏

4 How did you sleep last night? Indicate to what extent the following three statements apply to you.

	completely true	true	neutral	untrue	not true at all
I found it hard to get to sleep.	1	2	3	4	5
I suffered disturbed or broken sleep.	1	2	3	4	5
I awoke too early.	1	2	3	4	5

5 **Event** Did anything particular happen today which made you start to worry? If so then write down what happened below, using key words.

....

....

....

....

....

....

....

....

....

....

28
27
26
25
24
23
22
21
20
19
18
17
16
15
14
13
12
11
10
9
8
7
6
5
4
3
2
1

Day 5 *Talking about worrying*

Worry time I
Talking about worrying
morning/afternoon

Explanation   Worries have the unpleasant habit of entering your head and not leaving. These thoughts go round in circles and end up making things seem much worse than they really are. But you can get relief from this by saying your thoughts out loud. This is not to resolve your worries but rather to share them and unload them.

Week

1

a   Begin with around ten minutes intense worrying.

b   For the following exercise you will need someone who will listen to you. This can be anyone – a friend, acquaintance or parent. We shall call him/her X.

Today you will do the following: telephone the chosen person, talk to him/her or visit him/her. Ask this person if he/she has time to listen to you. Then recount a number of the worrying thoughts which are on your mind. Even if they appear to be insignificant, just express them out loud. For example: 'I am worried about my work.' You are expressing your worry. Just ask the person you have chosen to listen and not to offer solutions or advice. What you are doing here is expressing your worries and not solving them. This exercise is called talking about worrying. The objective is that in the meanwhile you now have someone in mind and that you carry out this exercise today.

In the meantime   Carry out the exercise of the first worry time. Get in touch with X.

Worry time II
Talking about worrying in your imagination
evening

Explanation   This exercise is handy for when there is no suitable
person available. The principle is the same as that used earlier
today.

a   Begin with five minutes intense worrying.

b   Did you manage to tell anyone your thoughts today? In the
following exercise you will once again talk about your worries.
But now we won't need anyone. You will do the same as in the
previous worry time but in your imagination. You will act as
though the person with whom you talked in the previous
exercise was sitting in front of you. Now once again talk about
the worries concerning you. They can be the same as those
from this morning or this afternoon but of course they don't
have to be.

At night   While undressing for bed, imagine that your clothes are
your worries. Take these off one after the other. Think about
your worries. With each piece of clothing you take off
consciously lay aside one worry.

Day 5 Notes

1 Tick the boxes to indicate which subjects you have worried about today (you can give several answers).

studies/ work	finances	health	relationships	family/ friends	what others think of me	other
❏	❏	❏	❏	❏	❏	❏

2 Tick a box to indicate how many minutes/hours you have worried today.

0–30 minutes	30–60 minutes	1–2 hours	2–3 hours	3–4 hours	4–5 hours	› 5 hours
❏	❏	❏	❏	❏	❏	❏

3 Tick a box to indicate how much effort it took today to stop worrying, on a scale of 1 (almost no effort) to 5 (a great deal of effort).

no effort at all	almost no effort	some effort	quite a lot of effort	a great deal of effort
❏	❏	❏	❏	❏

4 How did you sleep last night? Indicate to what extent the following three statements apply to you.

	completely true	true	neutral	untrue	not true at all
I found it hard to get to sleep.	1	2	3	4	5
I suffered disturbed or broken sleep.	1	2	3	4	5
I awoke too early.	1	2	3	4	5

5 **Event** Did anything particular happen today which made you start to worry? If so then write down what happened below, using key words.

....

....

....

....

....

....

....

....

....

Day 6 *Relaxation*

Worry time I
Muscle relaxation (arms)
morning/afternoon

Explanation   Worrying every day creates a great deal of tension and stress in your body. So today we are going to do some relaxation exercises so as to reduce this. Relaxation exercises are used to reduce physical complaints caused by worrying. They take away the feelings of tension in your body.

Week
1

a   Begin with ten minutes intense worrying.

b   Now we are going to do some relaxation exercises.
   Begin with your writing arm. Place your elbow on the arm of the chair, clench your fist and then tense your forearm and the biceps/upper arm. But don't overdo it – the aim is not to get cramp, it should stay feeling good. Keep the arm tensed for six seconds. Then say to yourself, 'Relax' and let your muscles go. Let your muscle relax for about ten seconds. Then repeat with the other arm.
   Tense the muscles for six seconds again. Say to yourself, 'Relax' and then relax this arm for about ten seconds.
   Repeat this exercise five times.

In the meantime   Try the talking in your imagination exercise. Or do the whirling exercise. You could also look for some distraction.

Worry time II
Muscle relaxation (legs)
evening

a   Begin with five minutes worrying.

b   Go and sit up straight on a chair and raise your right leg.
Stretch your leg out in front of you with the foot turned
inwards so that your big toe is pointing at your face. Do this
for six seconds. Say to yourself, 'Relax' and then put your leg
down again. Then do the same with the left leg. Repeat five
times.

At night   Try the relaxation exercises when lying in bed. Or do a
whirling exercise or a positive worrying exercise.

28
27
26
25
24
23
22
21
20
19
18
17
16
15
14
13
12
11
10
9
8
7
6
5
4
3
2
1

Day 6 Notes

1 Tick the boxes to indicate which subjects you have worried about today (you can give several answers).

studies/ work	finances	health	relationships	family/ friends	what others think of me	other
❑	❑	❑	❑	❑	❑	❑

2 Tick a box to indicate how many minutes/hours you have worried today.

0–30 minutes	30–60 minutes	1–2 hours	2–3 hours	3–4 hours	4–5 hours	› 5 hours
❑	❑	❑	❑	❑	❑	❑

3 Tick a box to indicate how much effort it took today to stop worrying, on a scale of 1 (almost no effort) to 5 (a great deal of effort).

no effort at all	almost no effort	some effort	quite a lot of effort	a great deal of effort
❑	❑	❑	❑	❑

4 How did you sleep last night? Indicate to what extent the following three statements apply to you.

	completely true	true	neutral	untrue	not true at all
I found it hard to get to sleep.	1	2	3	4	5
I suffered disturbed or broken sleep.	1	2	3	4	5
I awoke too early.	1	2	3	4	5

5 **Event** Did anything particular happen today which made you start to worry? If so then write down what happened below, using key words.

....

....

....

....

....

....

....

....

....

....

28
27
26
25
24
23
22
21
20
19
18
17
16
15
14
13
12
11
10
9
8
7
6
5
4
3
2
1

Day 7 I must = I want to

Worry time I
I must = I want to
morning/afternoon

a Begin with five minutes intense worrying.

b When you go through what you have wanted to do in the day
ahead, are you perhaps inclined to set yourself tasks such as:
'I still have to . . . And after that I must . . .'? These self-
imposed obligations are enough to give you a headache. For
this reason you have to tell yourself that you don't *have to* do
certain things but that you *want* to do them. Think about the
things you *must* do today and then tell yourself that you don't
have to do them but that you *want to* do them. You are going
to do the following exercise. Every time you use the words
must or *have to* in your thoughts today replace it straightaway
with the words '*I want*'. For example, you should replace 'I
must go to training today' with 'No, I don't *have to* go to
training at all but *I want* to go to training because *I want* to
stay fit and healthy.'

In the meantime Try to put off worrying thoughts until the next
worry time. If this does not work, then look for some
distraction or do one of the relaxation exercises.

Worry time II
Breathing from the stomach
evening

Explanation   Breathing from the stomach kills two birds with one stone. First, the tension caused by worry will be reduced. Second, concentrating on breathing will distract you.

a   Begin with ten minutes intense worrying.

b   A good exercise to relax you is to pay attention to your breathing. The following exercise will teach you to relax by making better use of your breathing.

   Go and sit or lie as comfortably as possible in a comfy chair or on the sofa. Place one or two hands on your stomach. You can also close your eyes if you like. Breathe in deeply through your nose. Try to feel the movement of your stomach. Don't hold your breath, just breathe out quietly.

   Try to breathe out for longer than you breathe in. What is important is that you are breathing in a quiet and relaxed manner. Don't do this for longer than a few minutes.

At night   You may be tossing and turning with worry all the more due to the tension you are feeling. Try to postpone your worries until the next worry time. Use the distraction, positive worrying exercise 1 or positive worrying exercise 2.

28
27
26
25
24
23
22
21
20
19
18
17
16
15
14
13
12
11
10
9
8
7
6
5
4
3
2
1

Day 7 Notes

1   Tick the boxes to indicate which subjects you have worried about today (you can give several answers).

studies/ work	finances	health	relationships	family/ friends	what others think of me	other
❑	❑	❑	❑	❑	❑	❑

2   Tick a box to indicate how many minutes/hours you have worried today.

0–30 minutes	30–60 minutes	1–2 hours	2–3 hours	3–4 hours	4–5 hours	> 5 hours
❑	❑	❑	❑	❑	❑	❑

3   Tick a box to indicate how much effort it took today to stop worrying, on a scale of 1 (almost no effort) to 5 (a great deal of effort).

no effort at all	almost no effort	some effort	quite a lot of effort	a great deal of effort
❑	❑	❑	❑	❑

4 How did you sleep last night? Indicate to what extent the following three statements apply to you.

	completely true	true	neutral	untrue	not true at all
I found it hard to get to sleep.	1	2	3	4	5
I suffered disturbed or broken sleep.	1	2	3	4	5
I awoke too early.	1	2	3	4	5

5 **Event** Did anything particular happen today which made you start to worry? If so then write down what happened below, using key words.

....

....

....

....

....

....

....

....

....

....

28
27
26
25
24
23
22
21
20
19
18
17
16
15
14
13
12
11
10
9
8
7
6
5
4
3
2
1

How much have you worried over the past week?

For each of the following statements indicate which is most applicable to you by circling the appropriate number. This applies to the past week.

		never	very rarely	rarely	some-times	often	very often	almost always
1	If I did not have enough time to do everything, I did not worry about it.	6	5	4	3	2	1	0
2	My worries overwhelmed me.	0	1	2	3	4	5	6
3	I didn't tend to worry about things.	6	5	4	3	2	1	0
4	Many situations made me worry.	0	1	2	3	4	5	6
5	I knew that I shouldn't have worried about things but I just couldn't help it.	0	1	2	3	4	5	6
6	When I was under pressure, I worried a lot.	0	1	2	3	4	5	6
7	I was always worrying about something.	0	1	2	3	4	5	6
8	I found it easy to dismiss worrisome thoughts.	6	5	4	3	2	1	0

	never	very rarely	rarely	some-times	often	very often	almost always
9 As soon as I finished one task, I started to worry about everything else that I had to do.	0	1	2	3	4	5	6
10 I did not worry about anything.	6	5	4	3	2	1	0
11 When there was nothing more I could do about a concern, I did not worry about it any more.	6	5	4	3	2	1	0
12 I noticed that I had been worrying about things.	0	1	2	3	4	5	6
13 Once I started worrying, I couldn't stop.	0	1	2	3	4	5	6
14 I worried all the time.	0	1	2	3	4	5	6
15 I worried about projects until they were all done.	0	1	2	3	4	5	6
Total							

⟹ *Total score for the first week:*

Week
2

Day 8 *Worrying and writing worries down*

Worry time I
Writing down worries
morning/afternoon

a   Begin with five minutes intense worrying.

b   Now get out your pen and paper/notebook and spend ten minutes writing down your worries. For example: 'When I go to a party I am afraid that people won't like me.'

Week
2

In the meantime   Whenever you start worrying, write down your worries in your notebook, using key words. Postpone worrying thoughts until the next worry time.

Worry time II
Positive worrying, exercise 1
evening

a Begin with five minutes intense worrying.

b We shall spend the next five minutes on a fantasy exercise.
You're going to write this time too so get out your pen and
notebook. Sit in a relaxed position. Close your eyes and take a
couple of deep breaths. Go back in your thoughts to an event
which at the time made you happy. Think about this as hard as
you can. Look around you in your thoughts and pay attention
to the small things.

What colours did you see? What kind of noises were there
to be heard? Who was there? What did they say? What could
you smell at that moment? Go back to this event in your
thoughts for five minutes. Now write about this event.

At night If necessary, open the old shoebox/rucksack. You should
still have the old shoebox/rucksack under the bed. Every time
you are awake and worrying put these worries in your
imagination into the box or the rucksack and put it back under
the bed. Then you can get out your worries again the following
morning.

Day 8 Notes

1   Tick the boxes to indicate which subjects you have worried
    about today (you can give several answers).

studies/ work	finances	health	relationships	family/ friends	what others think of me	other
❑	❑	❑	❑	❑	❑	❑

Week

2

2   Tick a box to indicate how many minutes/hours you have
    worried today.

0–30 minutes	30–60 minutes	1–2 hours	2–3 hours	3–4 hours	4–5 hours	> 5 hours
❑	❑	❑	❑	❑	❑	❑

3   Tick a box to indicate how much effort it took today to stop
    worrying, on a scale of 1 (almost no effort) to 5 (a great deal
    of effort).

no effort at all	almost no effort	some effort	quite a lot of effort	a great deal of effort
❑	❑	❑	❑	❑

4 How did you sleep last night? Indicate to what extent the following three statements apply to you.

	completely true	true	neutral	untrue	not true at all
I found it hard to get to sleep.	1	2	3	4	5
I suffered disturbed or broken sleep.	1	2	3	4	5
I awoke too early.	1	2	3	4	5

5 **Event** Did anything particular happen today which made you start to worry? If so then write down what happened below, using key words.

....

....

....

....

....

....

....

....

....

Day 9 *Top 3*

Worry time I
Top 3
morning/afternoon

a Begin again with around ten minutes intense worrying.

b Now go through the things you worry about frequently. Write down your top 3 worries on paper, putting the thing you worry about most frequently in the number 1 position.

c Note down this top 3 on the next page of this book.

In the meantime Try to postpone worrying thoughts until the next worry time. If this does not work then look for distraction or do one of the exercises which you have done up to now.

Worry time II
Positive worrying, exercise 2
evening

a Begin with around five minutes intense worrying.

b Now close your eyes. Think about something that you are good at. This can be anything. You stood up for yourself or someone else once, you are a good spouse, parent, colleague or friend, you are a good cook, you can write or dance well, you are amusing, smart. You are proud and you should then say to yourself: 'I am good at . . . and I am proud of that.' Perhaps you will doubt that you can hold onto this good feeling. So say it again: 'I am good at . . .' Now say it to yourself twenty times. Allow yourself to be proud for five minutes.

Sometimes you may not be able to worry intensely during the worry slot but this is nothing to be concerned about. Go through the other exercises as usual. Then try to worry intensely during the following worry time.

At night   Try to do the relaxation exercises when you are in bed.

Top 3 worries

1   ....

   ....

   ....

2   ....

   ....

   ....

3   ....

   ....

   ....

28
27
26
25
24
23
22
21
20
19
18
17
16
15
14
13
12
11
10
9
8
7
6
5
4
3
2
1

Day 9 Notes

1   Tick the boxes to indicate which subjects you have worried
    about today (you can give several answers).

studies/ work	finances	health	relationships	family/ friends	what others think of me	other
❑	❑	❑	❑	❑	❑	❑

Week

2

2   Tick a box to indicate how many minutes/hours you have
    worried today.

0–30 minutes	30–60 minutes	1–2 hours	2–3 hours	3–4 hours	4–5 hours	› 5 hours
❑	❑	❑	❑	❑	❑	❑

3   Tick a box to indicate how much effort it took today to stop
    worrying, on a scale of 1 (almost no effort) to 5 (a great deal
    of effort).

no effort at all	almost no effort	some effort	quite a lot of effort	a great deal of effort
❑	❑	❑	❑	❑

4 How did you sleep last night? Indicate to what extent the following three statements apply to you.

	completely true	true	neutral	untrue	not true at all
I found it hard to get to sleep.	1	2	3	4	5
I suffered disturbed or broken sleep.	1	2	3	4	5
I awoke too early.	1	2	3	4	5

5 **Event** Did anything particular happen today which made you start to worry? If so then write down what happened below, using key words.

....

....

....

....

....

....

....

....

....

Day 10 *Positive future*

Worry time I
Positive future alternative
morning/afternoon

a Begin with around ten minutes intense worrying.

b Now look at your most significant worries like a film. Next write down an extremely positive alternative to these thoughts. Try to make the situation exactly as you want it. Use your imagination and try to make it as lifelike as possible. You can exaggerate, however odd your ideas may seem. For example: 'Tomorrow (next week) when I am at the party people will compliment me on my good taste in clothes. They will say I look amazing. Everyone will want to talk to me and they will think I have something interesting to say. I feel completely at home. The atmosphere is really good.'

In the meantime Have you been worrying a lot over the day? Clap your hands and say to yourself, 'Not now!' Try to keep your worries for the following worry time.

Worry time II
Your choice
evening

Here choose the exercise which you have found most helpful up to now.

At night   While undressing for bed, imagine that your clothes are your worries. Take these off one after the other. Think about your worries. With each piece of clothing you take off consciously lay aside one worry. The following day you can put them on again.

28
27
26
25
24
23
22
21
20
19
18
17
16
15
14
13
12
11
10
9
8
7
6
5
4
3
2
1

Day 10 Notes

1 Tick the boxes to indicate which subjects you have worried about today (you can give several answers).

studies/ work	finances	health	relationships	family/ friends	what others think of me	other
❏	❏	❏	❏	❏	❏	❏

Week

2

2 Tick a box to indicate how many minutes/hours you have worried today.

0–30 minutes	30–60 minutes	1–2 hours	2–3 hours	3–4 hours	4–5 hours	› 5 hours
❏	❏	❏	❏	❏	❏	❏

3 Tick a box to indicate how much effort it took today to stop worrying, on a scale of 1 (almost no effort) to 5 (a great deal of effort).

no effort at all	almost no effort	some effort	quite a lot of effort	a great deal of effort
❏	❏	❏	❏	❏

4 How did you sleep last night? Indicate to what extent the following three statements apply to you.

	completely true	true	neutral	untrue	not true at all
I found it hard to get to sleep.	1	2	3	4	5
I suffered disturbed or broken sleep.	1	2	3	4	5
I awoke too early.	1	2	3	4	5

5 Event Did anything particular happen today which made you start to worry? If so then write down what happened below, using key words.

....

....

....

....

....

....

....

....

....

....

28
27
26
25
24
23
22
21
20
19
18
17
16
15
14
13
12
11
10
9
8
7
6
5
4
3
2
1

Day 11 *Negative future*

Worry time I
Negative future alternative
morning/afternoon

a   Begin again with around ten minutes intense worrying.

b   This exercise is the same as exercise b for day 10. But this time
     you will change your positive story into a negative one. Get out
     your pen and paper and write it down in as much detail as
     possible. What is the worst that can happen tomorrow (or next
     week)? Feel free to exaggerate here too. For example: 'I will go
     to the party and the people I meet there will not like me!
     Worse still, they will think I am a joke. They will not say a
     single word to me. People will act as though I am not there.
     When I want to say something I will be mocked or snapped at.
     They will be laughing at me behind my back.'

In the meantime   If you start worrying, then postpone this until
     the next worry time, look for some distraction or do the
     whirling exercise.

Week
2

Worry time II
Whirling exercise
evening

a Begin again with around five minute intense worrying.

b Empty your mind for the following exercise. If thoughts come
into your mind, don't try and prevent this. Thoughts are just
thoughts. Accept everything that comes to mind. Place these
thoughts in light clouds. Let these clouds quietly whirl around
in your head while you concentrate on your breathing. Let the
clouds with thoughts in them move here and there slowly in
your head, from left to right and back again. When you breathe
out you can quietly blow the clouds away. In this way you can
allow the thoughts to come and then go again.

At night Are you unable to sleep at night due to worrying? There
are a number of things that could help you. Before going to
sleep you could drink a glass of warm milk, read or listen to
music. This will distract you from your worries. Put on
something warm, for example pyjamas or an extra T-shirt.

Day 11 Notes

1   Tick the boxes to indicate which subjects you have worried about today (you can give several answers).

studies/ work	finances	health	relationships	family/ friends	what others think of me	other
❏	❏	❏	❏	❏	❏	❏

2   Tick a box to indicate how many minutes/hours you have worried today.

0–30 minutes	30–60 minutes	1–2 hours	2–3 hours	3–4 hours	4–5 hours	› 5 hours
❏	❏	❏	❏	❏	❏	❏

3   Tick a box to indicate how much effort it took today to stop worrying, on a scale of 1 (almost no effort) to 5 (a great deal of effort).

no effort at all	almost no effort	some effort	quite a lot of effort	a great deal of effort
❏	❏	❏	❏	❏

4   How did you sleep last night? Indicate to what extent the following three statements apply to you.

	completely true	true	neutral	untrue	not true at all
I found it hard to get to sleep.	1	2	3	4	5
I suffered disturbed or broken sleep.	1	2	3	4	5
I awoke too early.	1	2	3	4	5

5   **Event**   Did anything particular happen today which made you start to worry? If so then write down what happened below, using key words.

....

....

....

....

....

....

....

....

....

28
27
26
25
24
23
22
21
20
19
18
17
16
15
14
13
12
11
10
9
8
7
6
5
4
3
2
1

Day 12 *Probable future*

Worry time I
Probable future alternative
morning/afternoon

Explanation   When you worry about what the future may hold, do you have a realistic picture of It? Or is this picture of the future overshadowed by negative thoughts and feelings? This exercise will help you to put your thoughts in perspective, relax and learn to view the future positively.

Week
2

a   Begin again with around ten minutes intense worrying.

b   We shall go further with future expectations. Over the last couple of days you have written down the most positive and the most negative scenarios for a day in the near future. There is still one more expectation of the future. Now write down the future scenario which is mid-way between the worst case and best case scenarios. This is probably the most realistic scenario.

In the meantime   Try to postpone worrying thoughts until the next worry time. If this does not work, then look for some distraction or do one of the exercises which you have done up to now.

Worry time II
Whirling exercise
evening

a   Begin with around five minutes worrying. Worry as intensely as possible.

b   We shall go further with a whirling exercise. Let the thoughts come. Thoughts are not reality. There are no bad thoughts. You don't have to think the thoughts. You can let them be what they are. You don't have to concentrate on the thoughts, you can let them whirl away too. You don't have to finish your thoughts. You don't need to control your thoughts. Put them in little clouds. We call this thought whirling.

At night   You may be tossing and turning with worry all the more due to the tension you are feeling. Try to postpone your worries until the next worry time. Think about the 'I must = I want to' exercise!

28
27
26
25
24
23
22
21
20
19
18
17
16
15
14
13
12
11
10
9
8
7
6
5
4
3
2
1

Day 12 Notes

1   Tick the boxes to indicate which subjects you have worried about today (you can give several answers).

studies/ work	finances	health	relationships	family/ friends	what others think of me	other
❑	❑	❑	❑	❑	❑	❑

Week

2

2   Tick a box to indicate how many minutes/hours you have worried today.

0–30 minutes	30–60 minutes	1–2 hours	2–3 hours	3–4 hours	4–5 hours	› 5 hours
❑	❑	❑	❑	❑	❑	❑

3   Tick a box to indicate how much effort it took today to stop worrying, on a scale of 1 (almost no effort) to 5 (a great deal of effort).

no effort at all	almost no effort	some effort	quite a lot of effort	a great deal of effort
❑	❑	❑	❑	❑

4 How did you sleep last night? Indicate to what extent the following three statements apply to you.

	completely true	true	neutral	untrue	not true at all
I found it hard to get to sleep.	1	2	3	4	5
I suffered disturbed or broken sleep.	1	2	3	4	5
I awoke too early.	1	2	3	4	5

5 **Event** Did anything particular happen today which made you start to worry? If so then write down what happened below, using key words.

....

....

....

....

....

....

....

....

....

Day 13 *The next time*

Worry time I
The next time
morning/afternoon

Explanation   We often waste a lot of time and energy brooding over past events, blaming ourselves for not handling things better. In this exercise you will learn how to react next time so that you are less affected by worry. So instead of brooding about what has happened you can come to a solution: you will be thinking constructively.

Week

2

a   Begin now with around five minutes intense worrying.

b   The exercise deals with the choices you have made which you were dissatisfied with afterwards. In most cases worrying about the past involves the question 'why?'. For example, 'Why didn't I say no to that request?' These why questions can be very exhausting. Can you recall being in a situation like this?
    Get a pen and paper and write down how you want to react in a similar situation in the future.

In the meantime   When you are worrying a lot, write down your worries in the form of keywords. Then work on these in the next worry time.

Worry time II
Breathing from the stomach
evening

a Begin with around ten minutes intense worrying.

b Now we are going to do a breathing exercise. Paying attention
to your breathing is a good way to relax. The following exercise
will teach you to relax by making better use of your breathing.
Go and sit or lie as comfortably as possible in a comfy
chair or on the sofa. Place one or two hands on your stomach.
You can also close your eyes if you like. Breathe in deeply
through your nose. Try to feel the movement of your stomach.
Don't hold your breath, just breathe out quietly. Try to breathe
out for longer than you breathe in. What is important is that
you are breathing in a quiet and relaxed manner. Don't do this
for longer than a few minutes.

At night Try the breathing from the stomach exercise once at
night too.

28
27
26
25
24
23
22
21
20
19
18
17
16
15
14
13
12
11
10
9
8
7
6
5
4
3
2
1

Day 13 Notes

1   Tick the boxes to indicate which subjects you have worried
    about today (you can give several answers).

studies/ work	finances	health	relationships	family/ friends	what others think of me	other
❏	❏	❏	❏	❏	❏	❏

2   Tick a box to indicate how many minutes/hours you have
    worried today.

0–30 minutes	30–60 minutes	1–2 hours	2–3 hours	3–4 hours	4–5 hours	› 5 hours
❏	❏	❏	❏	❏	❏	❏

3   Tick a box to indicate how much effort it took today to stop
    worrying, on a scale of 1 (almost no effort) to 5 (a great deal
    of effort).

no effort at all	almost no effort	some effort	quite a lot of effort	a great deal of effort
❏	❏	❏	❏	❏

4 How did you sleep last night? Indicate to what extent the following three statements apply to you.

	completely true	true	neutral	untrue	not true at all
I found it hard to get to sleep.	1	2	3	4	5
I suffered disturbed or broken sleep.	1	2	3	4	5
I awoke too early.	1	2	3	4	5

5 **Event** Did anything particular happen today which made you start to worry? If so then write down what happened below, using key words.

....

....

....

....

....

....

....

....

....

....

28
27
26
25
24
23
22
21
20
19
18
17
16
15
14
13
12
11
10
9
8
7
6
5
4
3
2
1

Day 14 *Catch thoughts when relaxed*

Worry time I
Catching mice
morning/afternoon

Try to relax. Imagine that you are a cat out hunting for mice. You are lying next to a mouse hole in the skirting board, waiting for any mouse that may poke his head out so that you can then pounce on him. You are the cat. As soon as a mouse looks out, jump on the mouse and catch him with your paws. Now replace the mouse in your thoughts with a worry: as soon as another worry pokes its head out you will jump on this mouse and catch it with your paws. You can decide for yourself what to do with this thought afterwards. In this way you will teach yourself to be on the alert for those moments when a (known) worry appears. As soon as you become conscious that a worry has popped into your mind, then jump on this worry, grab it by the scruff of its neck and try to render it harmless. You can render the mouse harmless by, for example, shutting it in a box and then going on the lookout for new mice.

In the meantime Do one of the whirling exercises. Let your thoughts go and think: 'I don't *have* to, I *want* to!'

Worry time II
Muscle relaxation (arms)
evening

a Begin with around five minutes intense worrying.

b Now we are going to do some relaxation exercises.

⇒ Begin with your writing arm. Place your elbow on the arm of the chair, clench your fist and then tense your forearm and the biceps/upper arm. But don't overdo it – the aim is not to get cramp, it should stay feeling good. Keep the arm tensed for six seconds. Then say to yourself, 'Relax' and let your muscles go. Let your muscle relax for about ten seconds. Then repeat with the other arm. Tense the muscles for six seconds again. Say to yourself, 'Relax' and then relax this arm for about ten seconds. Repeat this exercise five times.

⇒ Then repeat with the other arm. Tense the muscles for six seconds again. Say to yourself, 'Relax' and then relax this arm for about ten seconds.

Repeat this exercise five times.

At night Try the muscle relaxation exercises when you are in bed.

28
27
26
25
24
23
22
21
20
19
18
17
16
15
14
13
12
11
10
9
8
7
6
5
4
3
2
1

Day 14 Notes

1   Tick the boxes to indicate which subjects you have worried
    about today (you can give several answers).

studies/ work	finances	health	relationships	family/ friends	what others think of me	other
❑	❑	❑	❑	❑	❑	❑

2   Tick a box to indicate how many minutes/hours you have
    worried today.

0–30 minutes	30–60 minutes	1–2 hours	2–3 hours	3–4 hours	4–5 hours	› 5 hours
❑	❑	❑	❑	❑	❑	❑

3   Tick a box to indicate how much effort it took today to stop
    worrying, on a scale of 1 (almost no effort) to 5 (a great deal
    of effort).

no effort at all	almost no effort	some effort	quite a lot of effort	a great deal of effort
❑	❑	❑	❑	❑

4 How did you sleep last night? Indicate to what extent the following three statements apply to you.

	completely true	true	neutral	untrue	not true at all
I found it hard to get to sleep.	1	2	3	4	5
I suffered disturbed or broken sleep.	1	2	3	4	5
I awoke too early.	1	2	3	4	5

5 **Event** Did anything particular happen today which made you start to worry? If so then write down what happened below, using key words.

....

....

....

....

....

....

....

....

....

....

How much have you worried over the past week?

For each of the following statements indicate which is most applicable to you by circling the appropriate number. This applies to the past week.

		never	very rarely	rarely	some-times	often	very often	almost always
1	If I did not have enough time to do everything, I did not worry about it.	6	5	4	3	2	1	0
2	My worries overwhelmed me.	0	1	2	3	4	5	6
3	I didn't tend to worry about things.	6	5	4	3	2	1	0
4	Many situations made me worry.	0	1	2	3	4	5	6
5	I knew that I shouldn't have worried about things but I just couldn't help it.	0	1	2	3	4	5	6
6	When I was under pressure, I worried a lot.	0	1	2	3	4	5	6
7	I was always worrying about something.	0	1	2	3	4	5	6
8	I found it easy to dismiss worrisome thoughts.	6	5	4	3	2	1	0
9	As soon as I finished one task, I started to worry about everything else that I had to do.	0	1	2	3	4	5	6

Week

2